365

DEVOTIONS

for

CATHOLIC

WOMEN

DAILY MOMENTS WITH GOD

Creative Communications for the Parish
1564 Fencorp Drive
Fenton, MO 63026
www.creativecommunications.com

365 Devotions for Catholic Women: Daily Moments with God
was compiled by Terence Hegarty, Kasey Nugent and Karen Tucker
for Creative Communications for the Parish,
1564 Fencorp Drive, Fenton, MO 63026. 800-325-9414.

www.livingfaith.com
www.creativecommunications.com

ISBN: 978-1-68279-248-3

Cover photo: Shutterstock.com
Cover design: Jeff McCall

Printed in the U.S.A.

Other books by *Living Faith* include:

365 Devotions for Catholics: Daily Moments with God

Living Faith: Prayers for Catholics

Reading God's Word

Living Faith Kids Sticker Booklets

Praying the Mass

Learning about the Sacraments

Praying the Rosary

Learning All About Mary

Meet Pope Francis

Meet Mother Teresa

Learning About the Ten Commandments

Praying the Stations of the Cross

What I See in Church

Living the Beatitudes

All About Angels

What We Do in Advent

What We Do in Lent

Learning About the Works of Mercy

Learning About the Bible

Heroes of the Old Testament

Heroes of the New Testament

TABLE OF CONTENTS

INTRODUCTION

**She is clothed with strength and dignity,
and she laughs at the days to come.** Proverbs 31:25

I doubt that you would have picked up this book had you not been influenced, in one way or another, by the Catholic faith. It's also safe to say that pretty much all of us have had our faith influenced by women in our lives. Whether your faith was fostered and strengthened as a child by your mother or grandmother or whether the example of a saint, a woman religious, a teacher or a public or historical figure inspired you, the powerful influence of women upon the world cannot be denied.

In fact, God's plan for the salvation of the human race depended wholly on the willing participation of a woman.

Mary's "yes" allowed our savior to be born. Her faith, her humility, her hard work and her suffering all played a crucial role in our being provided the opportunity, through Jesus, to walk through the doors of heaven. By presenting reflections that are written by your favorite *Living Faith* authors and are especially tailored to Catholic women, this book addresses the unique joys and challenges that women face in the world today. Those joys and challenges are celebrated here in a format that will both encourage you and strengthen you all year long.

I encourage you to, each day if you can, set aside some time for yourself and for God. That's definitely a challenge, since time to ourselves seems to be increasingly elusive in today's world. But if you can develop that habit, I'm confident that you will find inspiration and enrichment through the words of Scripture and the words of our authors, growing in your faith life and growing closer to God and neighbor.

And, as you begin this book, I am asking two things of you: First, promise yourself that when you get discouraged and miss a day or more, you won't give up. Do yourself the favor of picking up on the next day and continuing forward.

Second, please consider the people in your life who look to you as an example of how to live the faith. Someday, maybe a time far-distant from today, someone in your life will remember how you lived your faith. Consider, not only for your sake but for theirs, keeping this habit of growing closer to the Lord each day. I pray that *365 Devotions for Catholic Women* can play a part in that everyday development.

God bless,

Terence Hegarty
Editor, *Living Faith: Daily Catholic Devotions*

A PRAYER OF LOVE

Lord, if you tell me to love others just as You love them, then You must love them in me and through me. So the closer my union with You, the more I love all my sisters without distinction.

St. Thérèse of Lisieux

Mary: One of Us

And Mary kept all these things, reflecting on them in her heart. Luke 2:19

Today we celebrate not only New Year's Day, but also the Feast of Mary, the Mother of God, and the World Day of Peace.

In the chapel in our Provincial Center, we have a new life-sized statue of Mary that is unique. Mary is not standing stiffly. Rather, she is seated comfortably on a large rock. She wears no veil. Instead, her uncovered hair hangs loosely down her back. Her hands are resting on her lap; her feet are bare. Her facial expression exudes peace.

We have placed a chair in front of the statue. The chair invites people to sit down beside Mary when they pray to her. When I sit in that chair to pray, something happens to me. I experience a deep sense of Mary's oneness with me, with us. I find myself saying things like, "Hi, Mary! How are you today?" And I begin effortlessly to tell her how I am.

Mary, let me never forget that you are one of us. Please give me a reflective heart like yours!

Sr. Melannie Svoboda, S.N.D.

Resolve to Be More Forgiving

I am writing to you, children, because your sins have been forgiven for his name's sake. 1 John 2:12

There was a recent Christmas when I wrote to my adult children and said: "If there is anything I did to hurt you in any way, or anything you need to tell me that is bothering you, please let me know. I just don't want you to ever look back with regret and say: 'I wish I had said this, or told him about that time...'"

It produced a worried response. My daughter called me almost immediately and began with, "Whoa, Dad, what's happening?" It was the same for my son. I agreed it had an unintended funereal tone, but it was really meant to clear any roadblocks, to resolve any conflict, to heal any wound, to forgive and forget.

We aren't very good at forgiveness, either offering or accepting. This year, instead of a bunch of resolutions you will find hard to keep, call or write a loved one, mend a fence, seek forgiveness, offer your love.

Dear Jesus, teach me to forgive as you have forgiven us.

Paul Pennick

True
Self-improvement

Make straight the way of the Lord. John 1:23

How many people have already broken their New Year's resolutions? How many of us, despite our best intentions, have snitched a cookie or lit another cigarette already, or slept right through the time we allotted for prayer or exercise? And some of us, all too familiar with our frequent failures, didn't even bother to set goals this year. Knowing how often we have failed to straighten out our own lives, it's hard to muster the will necessary for the bigger task of making straight "the way of the Lord."

We have fallen short again and again. But no matter how often we have failed, God continues to stretch out a loving hand to us. Self-improvement should, at heart, be an effort to get rid of the things that distance us from God. It should be an attempt to become more fully the people God is creating us to be. This effort should continue whether we finally lose those ten pounds or not.

God, I am a work in progress. Help me straighten the way for you to come into my heart.

Karla Manternach

Teachable Moments

Children, let no one deceive you. The person who acts in righteousness is righteous, just as he is righteous. 1 John 3:7

More than a quarter of a century ago in January, my wife and I joyfully welcomed our fourth child, another healthy, beautiful baby girl to join her siblings. I knew that my newborn daughter would look to her parents as examples for many years to come. I wanted to display righteousness, to be a teacher for my children.

St. Elizabeth Ann Seton, whose feast we celebrate today, was also a teacher. In founding the Catholic school system in the U.S., she taught people about our Divine teacher, our "Rabbi," as Jesus was called. John the Baptist's two disciples saw Jesus and followed him, their teacher. They recognized that he was the Messiah and brought others to him.

I'm still learning and striving to be a positive example for my five adult children. Consciously or not, we are all imparting lessons. May we all attempt to teach others about the righteousness of Jesus.

Terence Hegarty

Divine Peekaboo

Why do you hide your face...? Psalm 44:25

Sometimes a mother plays a little game with her baby: She hides her face behind a blanket and after a few seconds, puts the blanket down and says, "Peekaboo! Here I am!" with a big smile. The baby laughs and mother hugs the little one. But if she stays hidden too long, the baby cries. Has mother really gone? We adults are in on the secret, so we enjoy the innocent surprise when she is found. We reassure the baby that mother was there all the time.

Often we act as if God hides from us. We can't see where God is acting in our lives, maybe because our problems obscure God's face. When good things happen to us, we can relate them to a loving savior. When difficulties surround us, we feel we are on shaky ground. Why can't we see the face of God?

Today perhaps we can find God's face in the sunrise or in a sunflower. Perhaps the face of a friend mirrors God's compassion. But perhaps I need to hold on blindly, believing that God's face is looking lovingly at me, although for some reason, I can't recognize it. Perhaps at this moment the face of God for me is the countenance of the suffering Christ.

Face of God, help me believe you are here.

Sr. Marguerite Zralek, O.P.

Light in the Dark Places

Great crowds from Galilee, the Decapolis, Jerusalem, and Judea, and from beyond the Jordan followed him. Matthew 4:25

Matthew is seriously into geography. Beginning with the infancy narratives, he is careful to include Jesus' location—Nazareth, Bethlehem, Egypt, back to Judea, a detour to Galilee. Jesus walked through the Holy Land without regard for borders, teaching and healing the chosen and the alien, clean and unclean, men and women. How ironic and how sad that the land of the Prince of Peace is one of the least peaceful places on earth, a land where living in harm's way is the norm and every mother's child is at risk.

Today is what my family calls the "real Epiphany." The tree comes down, and the ornaments and lights go back to the attic. As we celebrate the light that shone in the darkness, perhaps we can take heart to remember that the darker the place, the brighter the light seems. Let's bring light into the darkest recesses of our hearts and become an instrument of the peace for which this world longs.

Paige Byrne Shortal

A Timely Reminder

Stay awake, for you know neither the day nor the hour.

Matthew 25:13

Working in a long-term health care facility, I am reminded again and again of the value of life and the reality of death. They are not in tension, as if balancing a scale; I have come to see that God embraces both, equally strongly.

The words of the gospel do not have to be taken as a warning to impress us with fear. Nor do they apply only to life-and-death situations. Instead, they are a call to pay attention. They are a reminder not so much that God will show up when we least expect, but that we ought not lose a sense of expectation, a belief that God is present every day.

God is with us each moment, speaking to us through the dreams of our nights and the people of our days. Five of the bridesmaids in the story were wise to that. Five were not, so they missed out on the celebration. We do not have to. If we live each day with expectation and a believing heart, we will be ready for the presence of God.

May I live today not with "Where are you, God?" but with "There you are!"

Sr. Anita Constance, S.C.

A Dark Space Where God Dwells

> ...the priests could no longer minister because of the cloud, since the Lord's glory had filled the temple of the Lord.
>
> 1 Kings 8:11

This passage describes the arrival of the Ark of the Covenant in the Temple which was built for it. "Ark of the Covenant" is also one of the titles for the Mother of God because she allowed a space within her wherein God would dwell. She became a vessel which carried the covenant of love and communion between God and humanity. In this reading from 1 Kings, we learn that God chose to dwell in darkness: not the darkness of despair or anguish, but the darkness where life is created, as in the womb of Mary. The "ark," the space inside her where she welcomed her God, was carried within the "temple" of her own person.

So it is with us. We have inside us the capacity for God, the dark place, a place of fertility, kept for the Lord alone. We are asked, like Mary, to come to accept God in this place, not to run away (as we so often do). What would this look like? The reading says the presence of God was so overpowering that people had to stop what they were doing and just absorb the glory. Can you imagine?

Mary Marrocco

Starting Anew With God

In the beginning... John 1:1

The first of the year prompts us to make New Year's resolutions. Christmas vacations end. Work gets back to "normal." A new semester at school starts. Routine takes hold.

God is good at beginnings. In the beginning the Spirit hovered over the waters and God created the world. In the beginning was the Word and the Word was made flesh among us. In the beginning of our Christian life we were baptized, immersed in the water to die and rise with Jesus. Creation. Redemption. Sanctification.

In each case the people God chose to bless with his beginnings promised fidelity to the covenant God made with them. And in each case, including our own, we broke our promises and chose something other than God as the center of our life. God was always there to set things right, trying to catch our attention and to come back to him. Christmas is a welcome "retreat" in the midst of winter, a chance to realign our values, attitudes and behaviors. So this year, let this be your New Year's resolution!

Sr. Kathryn J. Hermes, F.S.P.

Christians Need a New Self

For neither does circumcision mean anything, nor does uncircumcision, but only a new creation. Galatians 6:15

Many of us experience a turning point in our lives, a time when we reassess old patterns of thought and action and find them wanting. At such times, we may recognize that we cannot move forward without undergoing radical change—a conversion experience resulting in a totally new self. Though this new self is always growing, from this moment on our energies seem to focus on inner realities instead of only on material goals. We discover that the meaning of life has more to do with the experience of peace and joy than with the state of our checking account.

For the Christian, there is another dimension to the creation of the new self. Ideally, we become mirrors of the Christ we profess to follow. The changes we experience reflect those qualities which are hallmarks of the Christian life. The works we accomplish imitate Jesus' own works of healing and teaching. In short, the new self involves nothing less than becoming the Christ-self, so that it is Jesus—and Jesus alone—who is the ground of our being.

Elizabeth-Anne Vanek

Praying and Purring

Like a weaned child on its mother's lap,
so is my soul within me. Psalm 131:2

In her book, *The Underneath*, Kathi Appelt describes a young cat purring. She writes, "Purring is not so different from praying...for in it lies a whole mixture of gratitude and longing, the twin ingredients of every prayer." Gratitude...longing...I like that comparison of praying to purring.

But why else do domestic cats purr? Some say purring is a sign of contentment and pleasure. But research shows that cats also purr when they are injured or in pain. Scientists speculate that perhaps those low frequency vibrations are part of a natural healing process.

Praying and purring. We pray when our hearts are filled with gratitude or longing. We pray when we experience contentment. But we also pray when we are injured or in pain, trusting that our very praying itself may be part of our healing process.

Healing Creator, help me to be faithful to prayer, no matter my circumstances. May I trust you enough to climb into your lap and just be.

Sr. Melannie Svoboda, S.N.D.

Avoiding the Urge to Deny Reality

For if anyone is a hearer of the word and not a doer, he is like a man who looks at his own face in a mirror. He sees himself, then goes off and promptly forgets what he looked like.

James 1:23-24

I find I do not enjoy looking into a mirror as much as I used to. Each day more wrinkles and blemishes seem to appear. The mirror confronts me with reality. James tells us the Word of God is like a mirror. We may think we are doing well spiritually—going to church on Sunday, giving some money to charity, minding our own business—but then the Scriptures confront us with some blemishes we had not noticed before. Now what?

James says we should not just turn away and forget what we saw. Rather, we should try to make our lives match what we saw. Sometimes I hesitate to look in the mirror because of what I might see, and sometimes I hesitate to look into the Scriptures for the same reason. But if I want to improve the state of my soul, I'd better take a good look at the word and do a spiritual makeover.

Lord, grant me the grace to peer into your word today and to bring my life into harmony with it.

Sr. Ruth Marlene Fox, O.S.B.

No Such Thing as 'Catholic Guilt'

**Though your sins be like scarlet,
they may become white as snow.** Isaiah 1:18

The guilt of sin can be crippling, immobilizing the soul from seeking forgiveness and reconciliation. A good friend told me once that he felt so burdened by guilt over a past deed that he couldn't seek God or faith or anything else. It was easier to give up and repeat the sin...which just led to more guilt.

Even though our sins may seem like a giant red letter hanging over our lives and guilt weighs us down to utter despair, we must come to know that, as Christians, we are called and empowered to rise above such feelings. There need be no "Catholic guilt" for us, for the work of forgiveness and reconciliation has already been done on our behalf. Our sins have been taken away. Guilt-free living is ours for the asking. There is a red more crimson than our scarlet sins, and that is the blood of Christ, poured out for us and for the forgiveness of our sins, creating a new life, clean and fresh and without guilt.

Jesus, you know my sins. Allow me to accept the forgiveness you offer so freely.

Steve Givens

The Worrying Thoughts of Mothers

Can a mother forget her infant,
be without tenderness for the child of her womb?
Even should she forget,
I will never forget you. Isaiah 49:15

I don't know how the parents of really large families cope, emotionally speaking. Because I've only got four children, and they've just about worn out my worry beads.

One seems directionless, another strikes me as a little too introverted, the next is a girl on the cusp of adolescence, which is self-explanatory, and the youngest is two, with legs that won't stop and a smart-aleck attitude. I could literally sit all day and worry about them. Really. But instead of worrying so much, I try to pray. And in that prayer, I do find comfort. But even more, I quietly settle myself and consider God's work for all of his children. God's love for us never fails, is never less than open, generous and forgiving.

God won't give up on any worrisome child. I can take comfort and strength from that as a parent—and, come to think of it, as a child as well.

Amy Welborn

EXERCISES IN TRUSTING

And when [Jesus] had said this, he said to [Peter], "Follow me." John 21:19

Before jobs and other circumstances scattered us, a group of my friends would gather every few months for a surprise night. Only the one planning the event knew where we were going and what we were going to do. Even with carpooling, this meant several cars following one another. We followed because we trusted that the person in the lead would not put us in any danger. To follow when we don't know what's ahead means being vulnerable and calls for trust. Yet for many of us, trust is difficult, even trust in God. To trust another, we must first share a loving relationship with that person. We cannot reveal our fears, doubts, hurts and other deep feelings to another unless we are certain that person cares enough for us not to take advantage of our vulnerability to harm us. To love to the depth of trust demands communication. That is what Jesus and Peter had. They knew they loved one another because they talked about it. We must do the same with those we love. It's important to tell God and others of our love for them and to hear of their love for us.

Charlotte A. Rancilio

Living in Truth Brings Lasting Joy

But they cried out in a loud voice, covered their ears, and rushed upon him together. Acts 7:57

St. Stephen is under attack here, and sadly enough, it is religious leaders who have covered their ears, unwilling to be confronted by truth.

Facing the truth can be painful, there's no doubt. There are times when the phone rings and I dread picking it up because I know it's one of my young adult sons, deep in a mess I can't fix. Or I see the look on my daughter's face when she comes home from school, and I think, "I can't. I can't hear about what mean girls have done to you today. It hurts too much and makes me too angry. Can't we just pretend?"

No, we can't. And if we're honest, we'll admit that we don't want to pretend. We know that the only real, lasting joy is in living in the truth.

Lord, give me the courage to face a painful truth today.

Amy Welborn

The Numbing Fear of Rejection

Everything that the Father gives me will come to me, and I will not reject anyone who comes to me... John 6:37

Rejection is one of the earliest experiences of pain we have, from seeing another child stick her tongue out at us to not being chosen for the team or getting an invitation to the birthday party of someone we thought was a friend. Later, we get "dumped" by dates, rejected by potential employers, not called back after an audition. Our emotional armor gets thicker, but too often, our eagerness to put ourselves out there, to leap into the fray, to join the dance wanes.

Jesus tells us he will never reject us. His arms are held wide in an eternal embrace; we have only to step into them. He chooses us for his team; we have only to join the game. He awaits us on the dance floor; we have only to hear the music and begin to move.

Loving Savior, I know you are waiting for me. Grant me the courage to step into your love.

Heather Wilson

Jesus, Our Light in Darkness

I came into the world as light, so that everyone who believes in me might not remain in darkness. John 12:46

A friend recently showed me a precious family heirloom: her uncle's miner's lamp. It was from the age before such lamps were powered by batteries. Her uncle's lamp was a small gray metal lantern—about 5 inches high—with a hook on it to secure it to his miner's hat. A gauge on the lamp warned the miner when the fuel was getting low. How important it was to have such a gauge! No one would want to be caught without light in the total darkness of a coal mine.

In a way, we can say that Jesus is our "miner's lamp." He illumines our way as we negotiate the darkness of human living. What darkness? Ill health, the death of a loved one, the loss of a job, the worry over a child or grandchild, the fear of violence, the ache of loneliness, ignorance, a difficult decision that must be made. How important it is to check the gauge regularly to be sure we have sufficient fuel to keep our light shining.

Jesus, you are the light of my life. Direct all my steps today.

Sr. Melannie Svoboda, S.N.D.

Cleaning Up

He must increase; I must decrease. John 3:30

Worthless stuff can take up a whole lot of room in our homes. And yet, we have those three-sizes-too-small slacks that we haven't been able to wear for five years. We keep that musty newspaper clipping showing we made the high school honor roll, that book everyone was reading that we could never bring ourselves to finish. Unless an object brings you joy, is used, or is something you want the next generation to have, what's the point of keeping it?

Worthless stuff can take up a whole lot of room in our souls too—bitterness over a long-ago betrayal, vanity about our looks or position or skills, fear about the future. As stuff increases, the room for the Lord decreases. Make this the day that you begin tossing the junk—no yard sale needed—to reveal the true treasure and savor anew the joy it brings you.

Lord, may the way I live reflect that you are the most important force in my life.

Melanie Rigney

Words for Troubled Hearts

Do not let your hearts be troubled... In my Father's house there are many dwelling places. John 14:1-2

This gospel reading is very special to me: it was the gospel my family chose for my father's funeral. We chose this gospel because we found it immensely consoling—especially those first words: "Do not let your hearts be troubled." When Dad died, our hearts were troubled—deeply troubled. We were troubled by the months of pain and uncertainty that had preceded his death. We were troubled by the loss of such a good man, such a significant person in all of our lives. We were troubled by our concern for our mother who had been married to Dad for almost 66 years. What would happen to her now? How would she survive without him?

Sometimes our expressions of faith coincide perfectly with what we are experiencing. Other times, our words at are odds with what we are thinking and how we are feeling. At such times, we must keep praying our words of faith, trusting that our experience, in due time, will catch up to our words.

Loving God, help me to keep praying words of faith even when my thoughts and feelings fall short of my words.

Sr. Melannie Svoboda, S.N.D.

Stretching Out My Hands for Help

> **...when you were younger, you used to dress yourself and go where you wanted; but when you grow old, you will stretch out your hands, and someone else will dress you and lead you where you do not want to go.** John 21:18

Most of us tend to look back on our youth as a carefree time. We recall wistfully how we couldn't wait to grow up, to be independent, to do whatever we wanted. Then we did grow up—and reality soon began to set in, not entirely as we have expected it to be.

When we enter into adulthood, our lives change drastically. We put everything on hold while our children need us. Later, we must begin doing whatever we can to make sure our own parents are safe and secure. Before we realize what is happening, we are being led in directions we had not planned for and where we didn't realize we had to go. Wherever we find ourselves on life's journey, whatever our age, we remain "children" who always need to stretch out our hands for help from God and others.

Lord, when the cares of my world overtake me, help me remember that I am still your special child.

Kathleen Furman

Infinite Love

> Then was fulfilled what had been said through Jeremiah the prophet:
> "A voice was heard in Ramah,
>   sobbing and loud lamentation;
> Rachel weeping for her children,
>   and she would not be consoled,
>   since they were no more." Matthew 2:17-18

Down through the ages, from Jeremiah's time to Matthew's to ours, has been heard the weeping of women for their children, lost through their vulnerability to sickness, violence, injury and other ills. All is summed up in the shocking image of young innocents slain in response to our Savior's birth into the world. This gospel text imprints on our hearts that these tears are precious to God, because the suffering women and children are immeasurably precious to him.

We read this text at our Project Rachel retreats, where women whose children have been lost through abortion take time to grieve, speak to God, heal and learn (or learn again) God's infinite love for them and all of us. Rachel will be consoled at last, for her children are entrusted to God's sure mercy, and so is she. These women, as John Paul II predicted (*Evangelium vitae* 99), become "promoters of a new way of looking at human life".

Mary Marrocco

THE GREAT JOY IN TRUST AND HOPE

For I know well the plans I have in mind for you, says the LORD, plans for your welfare, not for woe! plans to give you a future full of hope. Jeremiah 29:11

A friend of mine, abandoned by her parents while she was in high school, was living in her car. She was pregnant. Today, thirty years later, happily married with a beautiful home and two adult children, she says it was Jeremiah 29:11 that got her through that awful time. It gets her through today's challenges—the loss of friends and relatives, health issues and the other confusion that besets all of us here on earth.

Believing in that future of hope can set our weary minds at rest as well. We don't have to do it alone, not pregnant teenagers living in their cars, not single women in positions of corporate or governmental power, not moms scrambling for ways to keep their families fed. He has loving plans for us. And, if we listen carefully, he will guide us toward fulfilling them.

Thank you, Father, for loving me.

Melanie Rigney

LOVE CANNOT BE HOARDED

...the love of God has been poured out into our hearts through the holy Spirit... Romans 5:5

In Canto VII of Dante's *Inferno*, the Hoarders and Spendthrifts bump and shove each other with huge rocks, brawling and yelping at each impact. Self-indulgent in life, they shared a distorted attitude towards money; they are condemned to the same circle of Hell because they were either tight-fisted misers haunted by the fear of want or extravagant squanderers obsessed by the desire for more.

Moderation in love is not a divine hallmark. Unlike money, love cannot be hoarded because then it ceases to be love. Nor can it be wasted because the supply is limitless. Paradoxically, the more one gives it away, the more love one has. Instead of becoming poorer through spending, one actually becomes richer—so rich that the love one lives is nothing less than God's own inner life, the life of the Trinity.

Teach us to give away the love you have given us, O God, that we may receive more.

Elizabeth-Anne Stewart

Respecting Others Is Golden

Do to others whatever you would have them do to you.

Matthew 7:12

You probably recognize the words above. They have journeyed through many pages of history labeled as "the golden rule." Of course, there is nothing golden about these words in themselves. Like all good advice, the gold is revealed as the words become flesh in us.

Sometimes simple truths are most profound. Jesus is pointing out the very simple truth that everyone desires to be respected. Practice respecting others today. Whatever you focus on in another person always grows larger. To focus on something that annoys you is like having that person's flaw under a magnifying glass: it keeps growing larger. It works the other way as well: to focus on some lovely quality will make it, too, grow.

When you wake up tomorrow ask yourself, "How would I like to be treated today?" Then move through the hours treating others in this way. You may be happy to notice that some will probably return the favor.

Sr. Macrina Wiederkehr, O.S.B.

'DO SMALL THINGS WITH GREAT LOVE'

And whoever gives only a cup of cold water to one of these little ones to drink because he is a disciple—amen, I say to you, he will surely not lose his reward. Matthew 10:42

My favorite scene in the movie *Ben Hur* occurs when Jesus, the local carpenter, gives Judah Ben Hur, the Roman slave, a cup of water. Judah, in chains, is being dragged through Nazareth. The Roman soldier in charge forbids anyone to give Judah water. Ignoring the command, Jesus fetches a cup of water, and gives it to the thirsting slave. Angrily the soldier goes to whip Jesus, but when he looks into his eyes, something prevents him from beating him.

Being a follower of Jesus often consists of small acts. We express our faith ordinarily, not in grandiose deeds, but in simple, loving gestures—opening a door for someone, smiling at a stranger, standing in line at a wake, giving another driver a break in traffic, dropping our envelope in the collection basket.

As Mother Teresa so wisely counseled, "Do small things with great love."

Jesus, help me to do many small things today with great love.

Sr. Melannie Svoboda, S.N.D.

A Higher Form of Welcome

Mary has chosen the better part and it will not be taken from her. Luke 10:42

Traditionally, Martha and Mary have represented the active and the contemplative: Martha, the busy sister, stands for service, while Mary, resting at Jesus' feet, is the quiet listener. Martha, however, is not just "active," but resentful. She fulfills her duty, but treats it as a burden, letting everyone know she is inconvenienced and overworked. We can imagine her grumbling while she works, her negativity bringing a cloud over the gathering!

Mary, in contrast, is active in her listening. Her hospitality lies not in service but in focused attention. It is not a question of neglecting her guest or of failing to take care of his needs. Rather, she assumes the position of disciple, opening her heart to every word.

Hospitality is important, but it goes beyond feeding our guests. Martha's understanding of hospitality is limited to being domestic. Mary, on the other hand, knows that to receive her Lord in loving attentiveness is a higher form of welcome.

Come, Lord; stay with us that we might welcome you.

Elizabeth-Anne Stewart

Taking the Lead in Service

> Whoever wishes to be great among you shall be your servant; whoever wishes to be first among you shall be your slave. Just so, the Son of Man did not come to be served but to serve and to give his life as ransom for many.
>
> Matthew 20:26-28

Jesus, you have set such a beautiful example for us. You have given us a teaching about service that is relevant in any age. You have given us a revolutionary tradition about the essence of Christian leadership, which you explained when the mother of James and John wanted assurances that her sons would get a special political appointment in your kingdom.

You are with us as one who serves. You are our king, our leader, the head of the Church. You are the one with all authority. Yet you respond like a servant, whose menial duties are done with special care. Why? The answer seems clear. Because you love us. It's as simple as that. A wise man once said, "One can serve without love but one cannot love without serving."

Give us a loving heart, Jesus, so that we, too, may learn to be great by serving others.

James E. Adams

DOING GOD'S WILL

For whoever does the will of my heavenly Father is my brother, and sister, and mother. Matthew 12:50

Like most sons, I have some wonderful stories about my mother. What holds them all together is her faith and all she taught me about the life and joy that come from doing God's will.

In Jesus' time, people knew his mother and probably had remarkable stories about her too. What was most precious about her, as Jesus said, was her attention to doing the will of God.

Today, both my mom and Mary remind me to be grateful for anyone who has taught and nurtured me, "mothered" me into doing God's will.

And tomorrow? I'll be celebrating my mother's life, along with the many other "mothers" who have been rich blessings to me.

Fr. James Krings

FAITH GOES BEYOND CLEVERNESS

O woman, great is your faith! Matthew 15:28

Jesus was a sharp-witted debater. The gospels relate numerous incidents in which he escaped his opponents' verbal traps with a devastating comeback. "Let the one among you who is without sin be the first to throw a stone" (John 8:7). Some quip that he lost an argument only once—to the Canaanite woman who had asked him to heal her daughter. Jesus rebuffed her, with the explanation that his mission was to Jewish people. But she did not care about Jesus' missionary priorities. She cared about her daughter and she knew that Jesus had the power to heal. Within Jesus' refusal she found a reason for him to do what she asked—at least the dogs should get some scraps!

One can picture the smile on Jesus' face at her clever response. But he saw behind it more than cleverness, he saw faith. The woman would not give up, she would not be discouraged; she believed in him. Unfortunately, I am too much the opposite of the Canaanite woman— rarely clever, but often yielding to discouragement. The first problem is beyond my control. But the second, I could do something about.

Kevin Perrotta

PARENTING IS AWESOME WORK

Most blessed are you among women, and blessed is the fruit of your womb. Luke 1:42

In an era when many delay having children or choose not to have them at all, the idea of the fruit of a woman's womb being blessed is almost a foreign concept. Though few would want to return to a time when a woman's status depended upon motherhood, parents often find themselves unsupported. Many mothers find themselves penalized by their insurance companies for getting pregnant and criticized by their coworkers for jeopardizing promising careers.

Sadly, too many women are so overwhelmed by the "super mom syndrome," that they have little time to feel blessed. Caught up in the endless cycle of tasks and responsibilities, they seldom stop to ponder the great mystery of each birth. Just as Mary and Elizabeth conceived children who would change the world, so each pregnancy can result in the birth of a hero—of a Martin Luther King, Jr., a Mahatma Gandhi, a Mother Teresa. To be a parent is an awesome undertaking.

Bless all those who give birth, O God of Creation.

Elizabeth-Anne Stewart

FORGET-ME-NOT

Can a mother forget her infant,
  be without tenderness for the child of her womb?
Even should she forget,
  I will never forget you. Isaiah 49:15

This passage from Isaiah, which I have loved for years, recently opened even more deeply for me. Conversations with a niece during her pregnancy and early weeks with her first child brought back memories of pregnancy and infancy days with my children. I felt wonder that even though my youngest will turn 50 this year, each is still a "child of my womb." I have spent time replaying stages and seasons, treasuring so many unforgotten aspects of each of their lives, some aspects causes for celebration, others wrenchingly difficult. All of them are part of the unique journey of that person I once gave birth to. My heart kept filling with a profound tenderness with each memory. That God holds us—and each facet of our story—with that intimate cherishing brings me an almost tearful awe. It means so much to realize in our challenging lives how tenderly God loves us, *never* forgetting us.

Patricia Livingston

IF YOU LOVE, YOU WILL HURT

The child's father and mother were amazed at what was said about him. Luke 2:33

Sometimes we imagine Joseph and Mary had an "in" with God that enabled them to see into the future. Or we think they always knew exactly what to say or do—as if God had given them a script on how to be the parents of Jesus. But this line from Luke's Gospel indicates how little they knew. They were "amazed" by Simeon's words—suggesting they did not fully realize what they had gotten themselves into.

Simeon also has a special message for Mary: "And you yourself a sword will pierce..." These are sobering words. But in one way they can be said to any new parent—or to anyone who has reached out in love to someone else. Though love is filled with many joys and delights, it also exposes us to pain, grief and anguish. Simply put: If you love, you will hurt. The infant in Mary's arms will grow up to exemplify these words.

Faithful God, help me to persist in loving others despite the hurt it may entail.

Sr. Melannie Svoboda, S.N.D.

LOVING MYSELF AS I LOVE OTHERS

You shall love your neighbor as yourself. Matthew 22:39

Jesus assumes that we love ourselves. Some of us, having heard long lists of our faults and admonitions against selfishness from parents, teachers or others, may not be very good at loving ourselves. Jesus, on the other hand, does not tell us to love our neighbors instead of or more than ourselves. He says to love them as ourselves.

So how should we love ourselves? I think the love he intends us to have for ourselves is the love we have for children and others who depend on us. It's the love that makes sure they get enough rest, eat a well-balanced diet, have some work and some recreation on most days, stay home when they're sick and appreciate the good things about themselves.

We do this for our children to help them become good human beings. So won't it make us better human beings? If we practice loving ourselves, we might just have enough energy and self-esteem to reach out to our neighbors with real generosity.

Aileen O'Donoghue

NO SABBATH FROM DOING GOD'S WORK

Then Jesus said to them, "I ask you, is it lawful to do good on the sabbath rather than to do evil, to save life rather than to destroy it?" Luke 6:9

We all like to take a vacation or have a holiday from work. Jesus tells us, however, that there aren't any days off from doing God's work. Bringing God's love to others is a 24-hours-a-day, 7-days-a-week responsibility. Sometimes God's call doesn't seem to be a burden. Having given ourselves to God, we may at times be unaware that we are doing God's work. At other times, however, our load seems heavy, emotionally and physically—caring for a sick or dying loved one, working full-time while rearing children, reaching out to meet the needs of someone who is difficult, demanding or ungrateful. It is often at these times that we are most aware of our need to rely on God's strength to meet the task at hand. Our faith and hope in God, coupled with God's unconditional love for us, empowers us to serve one another each day.

Charlotte A. Rancilio

LOVE FOR REAL

Whoever eats my flesh and drinks my blood remains in me and I in him. John 6:56

Sometimes I prefer my imaginary ideas of people to their realness. I want to hold them at a distance and maintain presumptions about them that allow me to maintain a sense of self-satisfaction.

Jesus does the opposite. He sees our weaknesses and, rather than withholding himself in judgment, he comes to us directly in the flesh. His is a love that seeks out others. He desires to draw them to himself in a patient and generous way and to remain in a mutually beneficent communion.

I long to love others because of their realness and their need as opposed to loving because of imaginary qualities that might offer me something I lack. Love for the sole purpose of giving to the vulnerable, flawed and weak, rather than to be loved in return and shored up in my own weakness.

Elizabeth Duffy

COMPASSIONATE PRESENCE

For the one who is least among all of you is the one who is the greatest. Luke 9:48

The story goes that the mother of a little girl became quite concerned when her daughter was late getting home from school. Her daughter explained that she was helping her friend who dropped her dolly in the street and broke it. "But how could you fix Betty's dolly?" the mother asked. Her daughter responded, "By sitting down on the curb next to Betty and helping her cry."

Jesus' mission was to show compassion in the world, and ours is the same. We need, first of all, to see the doll our friend has broken. The greatest among us might keep on walking, fearful of being late for something or they might try piecing the doll back together. But sit down and cry with a friend? That takes empathy, compassion and our precious time.

Jesus, thank you for the friends you've sent into my life when I've needed them most. Help me to be that friend for another this day.

Sr. Mary Charleen Hug, S.N.D.

We Are Wonderfully Made

**Truly you have formed my inmost being...
I give you thanks that I am fearfully, wonderfully made;
wonderful are your works.** Psalm 139:13-14

This psalm is like a love letter written by God to all humanity. It describes a God who knows us intimately, loves us completely and breathes life into us at every moment. Even though there are things about us that God calls us to change, this psalm tells us that we are God's wonderful creation.

It is easy to say that God loves and created us all; it is more difficult to acknowledge that torturers, murderers and terrorists are created and loved by God as well. Though their actions are evil and abhorrent, God loves and sustains them. God knit them in their mothers' wombs. Such knowledge is beyond us, far too weighty for us to bear.

Loving God, you made all people in your image. Let this awareness beat in my heart when I come face to face with the evil actions of others.

Karla Manternach

I Forget the Largeness I'm Part Of

[Jesus] noticed a poor widow putting in two small coins.

Luke 21:2

Today a thunderstorm came over the lake: great chains of brilliant lightning cracking open a gray-blue horizon.

Last night, we looked up to an array of stars, untasted worlds flung across the dark sky, touching the edges of our well-trod earth.

Yesterday, I held a week-old baby, a tiny newcomer emerging out of the unknown into my arms. How small we are, and how easily we forget the largeness we are part of.

All is the Lord's, and all is contained in our God. Its unimaginable immensity is a drop of the ocean to the limitlessness that is God. Yet Jesus Christ, the One "in whom all things came to be," Lord and Master of the universe, bends low to notice two coins dropped into the collection by a most insignificant person. The greatness of his love is able to see and take in the love of a woman invisible to the world.

Lord, help me to become big enough to be present to the little ones who need me.

Mary Marrocco

GRACIOUS—AND DEMANDING—WORDS

All spoke highly of him and were amazed at the gracious words that came from his mouth. Luke 4:22

Some of those who were amazed by Jesus remained impressed and followed him; some liked what he had to say, but went back to their lives; and some were put off by his gracious words and joined in the persecution against him.

One might be put off by gracious words when the speaker doesn't live the message. As Ralph Waldo Emerson said: "Who you are speaks so loudly I can't hear what you're saying." For those of us who strive to proclaim the gospel—whether by preaching or parenting, writing or in song—the words are bound to outpace our actions sometimes. What can we do? Admit our limitations and seek forgiveness.

We may reject the words because they demand too much. We go to church and sing about love and peace and forgiveness and following Jesus, but who can live up to the message? Again, lest we become one of the persecutors or the fallen away, acknowledging the disconnect and seeking forgiveness is the way to go.

Paige Byrne Shortal

'To Do Your Will...'

**To do your will, O my God, is my delight,
and your law is within my heart!** Psalm 40:9

After having one child, my husband and I were told that we most likely would not be able to have another. Although we eventually had two more daughters, even several decades later I still remember my pain and disappointment. I also remember the overwhelming jealousy I felt when a friend easily conceived her third child.

I struggled for weeks with my emotions until one day I felt a tug to offer my friend the baby items our young daughter had outgrown. For some reason that action released me from my prison of resentment and jealousy.

Sometimes we may think of doing God's will as a burden or even drudgery, but the opposite is true. Although we may find it difficult to follow our best instincts, we will end up delighted by our new found freedom if we listen and obey.

Terri Mifek

Loving Extravagantly

The house was filled with the fragrance of the oil. John 12:3

Many of us, through choice or economic necessity, have had to learn to live frugally. We try to practice making careful, deliberate choices, conscious of their effect on both our own household budget and the implications for the larger world.

So of course we take notice and stand in awe of the contrast we see in Mary's grand gesture: anointing Jesus with a liter of perfume that must have blown nearly a year's income. Like the lives of the holy ones given over in love and service without calculation of the cost, Mary's dramatic act of extravagance filled the entire home, enveloping all those present and lingering on in memory. More, her seemingly wasteful act profoundly comforted a dear friend who at that very moment was courageously inching closer to the longest, most tortuous journey of his life. Even today, the fragrance of such a gesture remains among us.

Sr. Chris Koellhoffer, I.H.M.

A Question of Memory

I will never forget you. Isaiah 49:15

A friend I had not seen in some time told me about his mother's dementia before her death. It was never diagnosed as Alzheimer's disease, but that is what the doctors thought she had. Little by little, her memory began to falter. My friend told me about the heartache of watching the slow decline of someone who was so smart, so engaged and so loving toward her children. One remarkable thing he mentioned was that, despite his mother losing most of her short-term memory, she could recall past events with almost perfect clarity. "She would forget that she was talking to me on the phone, but she could remember my dad's service number from World War II and even all the camps where he was stationed," he said.

Sadly, even a mother's memory can be compromised, but God's memory is never impaired. No matter what we have done, how we have ignored him, how we have distanced ourselves from him, he cares deeply for us. He remembers us and loves us without limit.

The question is: Do we remember him?

Paul Pennick

Born Again

> No one can enter the kingdom of God without being born of water and Spirit. What is born of flesh is flesh and what is born of spirit is spirit. John 3:5-6

Each of my six kids was baptized within a few weeks of their birth. I was so caught up in the throes of new motherhood that I have only hazy memories of the two most important events in their lives—their birth in the flesh and their birth in the spirit.

Fortunately, in the Mass we relive our baptism again and again. We cross ourselves with holy water as we enter the sanctuary. We confess our belief during the creed. We repent of our sins, and in the liturgy of the Eucharist, the priest adds a dash of water to the wine that will become our spiritual drink—the Body and Blood of Christ in the Eucharist.

These rituals make spiritual realities visible, and they remind us that being born again is something we can do every day.

Elizabeth Duffy

MORE THAN A SHOULDER TO CRY ON

In his love for her Isaac found solace after the death of his mother Sarah. Genesis 24:67

When my mother died several years ago, my wife was there to help me through my grief. When my father died more recently, she did it again. But her presence in my grief is more than just a healing hand or a shoulder to cry on, as Isaac seemed to know. However important her presence was in my grief, it was her love that pulled me through. For love gives larger meaning to life—and even to death. When we are loved we have a reason to pull through, a reason to go ahead and grieve and then get on with life. Isaac found solace in his love for Rebekah because he knew that love would continue when the tears stopped.

That's surely one reason God gives us the important people in our lives—wives, husbands, mothers, fathers, brothers, sisters, children, friends. They are living sacraments of God's love for us, reminding us that love will be there when all else fades.

Lord, thank you for the people you put in our lives who can give us the solace we need in times of darkness and despair. May your love, shining through them, always pull us through.

Steve Givens

Let's All Be Amateurs

Your every act should be done with love. 1 Corinthians 16:14

The word *amateur* sometimes has a negative connotation. Amateurs are not very good at what they do, we think. Or amateurs don't earn money for what they do. But recently, I learned the etymology of the word "amateur." It means *for the love of it*. In other words, amateurs do what they do, not to prove their prowess or to earn big bucks, but mainly because they love what they do.

What a beautiful attitude to have toward the things we do—especially our work. Whether we're leading a meeting, cleaning a bathroom, cooking supper, taking care of a customer or client, or teaching a child, do we bring a certain level of affection to our work? If we do, it will show in our attentiveness, our facial expression, our tone of voice and in the words we use.

God of Love, help me to keep my "amateur status" in all the work I do today. May my demeanor show that I bring love and affection to whatever task I may be doing.

Sr. Melannie Svoboda, S.N.D.

Sheep May Safely Graze

My sheep hear my voice; I know them, and they follow me. I give them eternal life, and they shall never perish. No one can take them out of my hand. My Father, who has given them to me, is greater than all... John 10:27-29

As a parent, I am constantly reminded of the dangers facing my children today: careless or distracted drivers; unsafe or unhealthy foods; diseases and superbugs; bullies, predators and all manner of depraved entertainment. Add to that their personal weaknesses and limitations, and it's easy to see them as sheep in the midst of wolves.

I can't keep my children from harm any more than I can avoid my own suffering, but I trust that God would never allow his children to wander into destruction. Jesus, the Good Shepherd, guides and protects them—and me—through this life, giving us the good things of Creation for nourishment and strength and feeding us with his own Flesh and Blood.

Lord, may my children prosper by trusting in your power and listening for your voice.

Julia DiSalvo

MERCY ABOUNDS!

Sirs, what must I do to be saved? Acts 16:30

Paul and Silas are unjustly imprisoned, and the jailer is warned to guard them securely. Despite the fact that the prisoners are staked in an inside cell where escape seems impossible, an earthquake throws open the doors of the prison. The jailer assumes the prisoners have escaped and is about to kill himself, presumably to avoid torture, when Paul shouts that all the prisoners have remained. The jailer's immediate response is conversion.

Paul had mercy on the jailer, and mercy is a powerful weapon for good. When mercy is recognized and accepted, the recipient may be moved to a radically different life. Mercy makes clear that our life is not a sum of what we are missing, but of what we have been given. The recognition of mercy inspires gratitude and a desire to pay it forward.

Sadly, we often don't recognize the mercy offered to us—from God, from those who love us and even from those we casually encounter each day. Mercy abounds.

Paige Byrne Shortal

Choosing to Love

We love because [God] first loved us. 1 John 4:19

Popular culture gives us a romantic picture of people falling in love, as if some mysterious force causes an unavoidable mutual attraction. This romantic attraction is not the love described in 1 John. In fact, love is a choice. The choice we make to love someone does not taper off over time. We express our love by acting in the best interest of those whom we love. I have found that loving words or actions don't come easy when someone has hurt me. To remain "in love," I must continually make the choice to love.

Jesus' words and actions showed us the power of love to liberate the poor and the imprisoned. In loving others, especially our enemies, we are liberated from the narrow borders of fear and hatred. To love because God loves us, we become neighbors with all of humanity. To choose love is the first step toward peace.

Deborah Meister

The God of All Encouragement

> Blessed be the God...of all encouragement, who encourages us in our every affliction, so that we may be able to encourage those who are in any affliction... 2 Corinthians 1:3-4

Because we have been encouraged and comforted by God, we can encourage and comfort others. Probably all of us have experienced a truly affirming person—someone whose smile, touch or kind word has really lifted our spirits. We know what a difference those simple gestures make, especially when we feel burdened. We can make that difference for others at home, work, church or neighborhood. A surprise phone call, note or flower are all wonderful ways of encouraging others. Isaiah describes the Messiah as one who would not "break the bruised reed nor quench the flickering flame." We have all probably quenched a few flickering flames in our lifetime. But we also know how to fan flickering flames. If we could think of each person in our day as a flickering flame, especially young persons—our children and grandchildren, students, nieces and nephews—what a difference our smile, word or touch could make! Of such tiny deeds is the kingdom of God made visible daily!

James McGinnis

Fellow Citizens

So then you are no longer strangers and sojourners, but you are fellow citizens with the holy ones and members of the household of God... Ephesians 2:19

My friend from here in Alabama (where I live) and I happened to both be in New York City at the same time. We didn't see each other, but we figured out later that we'd been at dinner in different restaurants on the same block at the same time. I'd strolled right past her. In the lobby of a small hotel in another city, I overheard a teenaged girl reference my hometown—she was a friend of my daughter's. A woman who lives a block over from us, not only attended my high school that is a state and 200 miles away, but her brother was in my small (54-member) class. Stumbling upon these connections is fun and exciting, but they also prompt reflection. Sometimes, I look at others and the first thing I see are differences. What if that's not the way it is? What if I interacted assuming connection and relatedness, instead?

Amy Welborn

No Miracle at Home

Do not be afraid. Go on speaking, and do not be silent, for I am with you. Acts 18:9-10

A psychiatrist friend, whose many patients loved and revered him for his compassion and common sense, told me that when his daughter was a teenager, she would sigh and wish for "someone just to talk to." He also confessed that his son would often sneak down to the local convenience store to talk to the guy who worked the evening shift. Those we love the most are often beyond our reach.

St. Paul grew up a good Jewish man, a recognized expert in the law and faithful to its practice. Yet when he speaks to the Jewish community about Jesus, the fulfillment of the law and the prophets whom he has encountered in a most personal and convincing way, he is rejected, even threatened. Ultimately, Paul is led to share the gospel with the Gentile community.

When we feel the pain of rejection by those we love, let's remember Paul and make of our lives a witness to the gospel for our loved ones and all on our path.

Paige Byrne Shortal

Put Them Away

> But now you must put them all away: anger, fury, malice, slander, and obscene language out of your mouths. Colossians 3:8

While I'm not proud to admit it, there have been times in my life when I was angry with God. Surely, had he wanted to, God could've prevented what I perceived to be injustices. I have been angry that a loved one was taken from this life far too soon (in my opinion). I have questioned why babies are born addicted to drugs, suffering terribly as they go through withdrawal. I wonder why people who have clearly committed evil acts are seemingly rewarded.

With faith and some perspective, we can begin to understand that such anger is a byproduct of earthly logic. And yet, the anger can persist. Today, may we endeavor to do as our reading encourages and put our anger, among other things, away, allowing ourselves to be renewed.

God of Justice, quell my anger and help me to trust that the only true justice is divine justice.

Terence Hegarty

A STRONG, LIVING FAITH

**Unless your faith is firm
you shall not be firm!** Isaiah 7:9

Nature offers an abundance of telling examples of the need for firm foundations. Trees grow their roots far into the ground so as to provide support. The roots provide water and stabilization, enabling the tree to stand firm in strong winds. A human fetus knows the secure and warm comfort of the mother's womb, a secure, firm and nourishing home. A baby is born and immediately is given still more firm foundations in the arms of its mother.

We need security. We cannot fully live without the comforting assurance of a strong faith. We may exist through our days and years bereft of faith, but when we are deeply troubled or our hearts are broken by loss or tragedy, we fall back on ourselves instead of God. We do not have within ourselves the sources to embrace life in its fullness. We need the Church, as given by God, as the source of a strong, living faith.

Fr. James Stephen Behrens, O.C.S.O.

AUTHENTIC, LASTING JOY

**Blessed are you who fear the LORD,
who walk in his ways!** Psalm 128:1

We may not all be mothers, as Monica was, but we all have had one. Our relationships with our mothers might be terrible or beautiful, or somewhere in an in-between place: bewildering, regretful and hopeful.

Desire lies at the heart of our mistakes and successes as parents, caretakers and children. Monica desired her son Augustine's salvation, and Augustine yearned for a love that would not die. Around and around they went.

What is it I desire for others? Is it that, above all, they find authentic, lasting joy?

Lord, may I be a help to others as we journey to you.

Amy Welborn

BEYOND THE DIRTY LAUNDRY

[Jesus] called his disciples to himself, and from them he chose Twelve, whom he also named apostles. Luke 6:13

When my sons were teenagers, we invited our pastor to dinner. He was given the tour, including their messy rooms (*shudder*), and afterwards he talked about how cool one boy's room was. I nodded, all the while thinking, "Seriously? That pig sty?" Later I went up to look and, for the first time, saw what our pastor saw. Every inch of wall and ceiling was covered with cartoons, paintings, quotes in calligraphy, his own photographs. It *was* cool. *(But what's with laundry on the floor?)*

I learned it's important to see beyond the dirty laundry. Consider how apparently ill-suited the Twelve were for the job of apostleship. Yet Jesus saw something in them. It is so important for potential to be noticed by the right person at the right time. This is perhaps the most significant job of the teacher, the counselor, the coach—or pastor or parent—making all the difference in an individual's life. Sadly, too often the very person in the position to do this important work is too busy about other matters—like laundry!

Paige Byrne Shortal

'Polite Prayer' May Not Be the Best

Unable to get near Jesus because of the crowd, they opened up the roof above him. Mark 2:4

These guys broke in through the roof to get to Jesus. And Jesus, instead of getting angry about the damage to the roof, granted their desire that their friend be healed. None of the many dear teachers and spiritual directors I have known would have approved of my breaking through the roof instead of waiting outside for my turn. Had I been in Capernaum with a friend seeking healing, I would have been polite. I would have waited outside, especially with scribes and other important people filling the house. I would have felt unworthy of interrupting those inside. I very well imagine carrying my friend away unhealed.

Jesus' reaction to those breaking in through the roof tells me that Jesus wants us to get to him any way we can and not to wait around being polite, not wait around until we're worthy, not wait around until we've read every book on prayer. Jesus wants us to break in through the roof, however impolite it feels.

Aileen O'Donoghue

Unexpected Grace

When his relatives heard of this they set out to seize him, for they said, "He is out of his mind." Mark 3:21

We want our lives to be rational and predictable; it makes us feel safe and in control. But from time to time, unexpected and seemingly irrational events occur beyond our comprehension and control. We then struggle to return to the status quo.

When Jesus burst upon the scene, people were challenged by his ministry and by his message. He threatened their view of the world and their lives. Some dismissed him, saying he was in league with the devil or that he was a blasphemer. His own relatives said, "He is out of his mind." But for those who were willing to let their lives be challenged and changed, he offered the grace of salvation.

God's grace often comes to us in seemingly irrational and unforeseen events. People have spoken to me of devastating events that eventually became sources of great grace: a lost job, a failed relationship or a personal illness initially seemed to be a terrible tragedy, but later was recognized as a moment of grace.

Consider what has unexpectedly happened to you in recent days. Has God's grace been manifest through this event?

Msgr. Stephen J. Rossetti

SUFFERING CAN INCREASE COMPASSION

Because he himself was tested through what he suffered, he is able to help those who are being tested. Hebrews 2:18

A teacher friend of mine was always a little harsh and impatient with her students. Then one summer she took a difficult graduate course and struggled immensely. Afterwards, she became a more understanding and patient teacher. A priest I know suffered with alcoholism for many years before entering a treatment program. He has not had a drink in more than nine years. Because of his experience, he became an excellent spiritual director. A nurse confided in me that after undergoing surgery herself, she was a more compassionate caregiver. Vulnerability can make us more approachable. Suffering can make us more compassionate. What draws many to Jesus are not his miracles, but his vulnerability and suffering. He truly became like us. Let us now become more like him.

Jesus, may my sufferings make me more approachable and compassionate—like you.

Sr. Melannie Svoboda, S.N.D.

AM I MEETING MY DEEPEST NEEDS?

I was hungry and you gave me food... Matthew 25:35

You might ask, "Have I adequately responded to those in need?" You might think of things like the meals you prepared for your family, the donations you made to the food shelf or the suppers you served at the homeless shelter. You may even gratefully recall the moments when you were truly able to recognize Christ in the lives you touched.

I suspect it's a little harder to acknowledge that Christ also lives within us. "Doers" can become so consumed with taking care of everyone else they forget they are also in need of nourishment. We may have a full stomach, but we can starve ourselves spiritually by not feeding our need for necessary things like solitude, beauty and recreation. Some of us have to be reminded that to admit we have legitimate needs is not selfishness but a healthy acknowledgment that we are not God or even angels.

Terri Mifek

MAY ALL KNOW GOD'S TENDERNESS

In their affliction, they shall look for me:
   "Come, let us return to the LORD,
For it is he who has rent, but he will heal us;
   he has struck us, but he will bind our wounds." Hosea 6:1

These words from the prophet Hosea were not what I wanted to read, having just returned from a tour of a newly-opened domestic abuse shelter. For the many women, children and sometimes men who have fled violent relationships, the image of a God who inflicts pain and then applies the bandages must be frighteningly familiar. I find myself wondering how I would explain Hosea's description of God to one of the mothers I met this afternoon, a survivor of years of abuse that began when she was a child. And then the Spirit fills my mind with images of a surgeon who must re-break a bone grown crooked, a fitness instructor who cajoles her class to complete "just one more set of exercises," a father who applies hot compresses to a daughter's ingrown nail. I pause and I pray for the families in the shelter, that in their pain, each of them may know the tenderness of God through the healing care of others today.

Claire J. King

EARLY EVANGELIZER

Jesus answered and said to her, "Everyone who drinks this water will be thirsty again; but whoever drinks the water I shall give will never thirst; the water I shall give will become in him a spring of water welling up to eternal life." The woman said to him, "Sir, give me this water, so that I may not be thirsty or have to keep coming here to draw water."

John 4:13-15

Preachers have used the line "you have had five husbands, and the one you have now is not your husband" to fit the Samaritan woman at the well into a sexist trope—fallen women saved from a life of sin. But the text doesn't support this. The past husbands likely died, and marriage statuses were complicated. Focusing on this unimportant detail allows them to dismiss the point, which is that that the Samaritan woman is one of the first evangelists. Her exchange with Jesus is lengthy and intelligent. Her questions and responses are direct and open. She seeks Divine Truth. Once she is convinced that Jesus is the Messiah, she goes back to her town to tell everyone. Many are converted. The Eastern Church calls her Photina and recognizes her as a saint, adding the title "equal-to-the-apostles," shared by several dozen figures responsible for great evangelism.

Jesus, give me this water, so that I may not be thirsty.

Phil Fox Rose

MARCH 3

BREAKING DOWN WALLS WITH LOVE

I have given you a model to follow, so that as I have done for you, you should also do. John 13:15

Mary Jo Copeland is the founder of Sharing and Caring Hands, a tremendously effective outreach to the poor in Minneapolis. The group runs shelters and transitional homes, day programs for teens and children and is generally known for being there to meet the needs of the poor, at any time. Every evening, Mary Jo ends the workday by taking out basins, filling them with warm water and then washing the feet of at least twelve people. She says that in washing feet, she is trying to share with the poor the reality of their own dignity as children of God.

These days are all about love. What Jesus has done for the disciples, he tells them, they are called to do for others. And what is that? It seems it might be to love, which is far more than kindness or good-feeling. Jesus, Son of God, reaches out through washing feet, through the sharing of his own Body and Blood, breaking down walls with love.

Jesus, Master, lead me in your way of service and love.

Amy Welborn

HINDSIGHT

And it happened that while they were conversing and debating, Jesus himself drew near and walked with them, but their eyes were prevented from recognizing him. Luke 24:15-16

She failed her exams but was given a second chance to get into the program of her choice. Even so, her eyes were prevented from recognizing him.

Once in college, she became entangled in a destructive relationship; eventually, after months of turmoil, she was finally able to break free. Even so, her eyes were prevented from recognizing him.

Distracted at the wheel, she drove recklessly at top speeds, inevitably crashing her car; she escaped without a scratch. Even so, her eyes were prevented from recognizing him.

Like the disciples walking to Emmaus, we can be so engrossed in ourselves that we fail to see the obvious; instead of recognizing the many signs of God's presence in our lives, we dismiss them, take them for granted or fail to see them altogether. What will finally open our eyes?

Open our eyes that we may see you walking beside us, O Lord, every day of our lives.

Elizabeth-Anne Stewart

'God Really Cares for Me'

Cast all your worries upon him because he cares for you.

1 Peter 5:7

My first day on retreat I spotted an ant on the sidewalk carrying a leaf many times his size. As I watched him struggling, I found myself saying to him, "I know just how you feel, buddy!" My spontaneous response to that little ant spoke volumes to me about where I was physically, spiritually and psychologically that particular day.

Paying attention to our spontaneous thoughts, feelings and words is a good way to begin to pray. Once we know where we are, we can begin to compare that with where we would like to be. Then we can pray for those graces we need to get there. If I'm crabby, for example, I may need the grace of patience, rest or gratitude. If I'm lonely, I may need to reach out to a friend or to someone in need. If I feel overburdened, I may need to renew my trust in the God who really, really cares for me.

Loving and caring God, help me to begin my prayer today by telling you where I am.

Sr. Melannie Svoboda, S.N.D.

Becoming Agents of Mercy

> What will happen to me there I do not know, except that in once city after another the holy Spirit has been warning me that imprisonment and hardships await me. Acts 20:22-23

God can lead us where we dare not go and make us agents of mercy in rock-hard places. I saw this truth emerge for a friend who accompanied a woman to dialysis every Monday evening for three years until her death. The procedure was physically agonizing for this blind, wheelchair-bound woman. In her youth she had escaped alone from Nazi Germany, making a new life in a country at war with her own homeland. Now this strong spirit was bound by bodily weakness. My friend, an agent of God's mercy within that well of pain and loneliness, had the courage to stand there with her in her final excruciating illness.

Here's a little glimpse of the spirit that led St. Paul to go where his heart directed him, even as he realized that imprisonment and hardship would be part of the journey. So it is with love, the love of Christ planted deep within us; it will not allow us be less than we are, but impels us to love even unto death.

Mary Marrocco

GROWING IN WISDOM

Then [wisdom] comes back to bring him happiness and reveal her secrets to him. Sirach 4:18

When I think of wisdom, I think of my mother. At 90 years of age she had buried not only her husband but both of her sons. Instead of defeating or crippling her, sorrow and adversity made her wiser and stronger. Like Mary, my mother was a rock upon whom others leaned. Not that she had a gift for pithy sayings or catchy phrases. Rather, her understanding heart and listening ear plus her deep love for God and her family endeared her to others. She was a person Sirach speaks of in this reading, a person to whom wisdom has revealed her secrets.

Wisdom is often associated with age, but not all elders are wise; some younger persons are very wise. I used to pray for wisdom and then I read something that made a lot of sense to me. Pray, yes, but if you want a particular virtue, "live into it." So if I want to be wise, I practice wisdom in my everyday dealings and then one day I find I have grown into it.

Direct my actions and thoughts this day, Lord, that I may grow in your wisdom.

Sr. Charleen Hug, S.N.D.

'FEASTING ON JESUS' PRESENCE'

I am the living bread that came down from heaven; whoever eats this bread will live forever. John 6:51

Bread is not the universal symbol we once imagined it to be. In fact, for some, it is simply not an option. In most African nations, yams, plantains, lentils and cassava are dietary essentials and wheat is a luxury import. In Asia, rice is the staple of the majority of the population of 4.4 billion. Even in the United States and Europe, gluten intolerance and the emphasis on low-carb diets mean that fewer and fewer people are consuming bread.

But while bread as a symbol has limited applications, Jesus is clear that he, himself is unlimited. Available to all as a source of spiritual sustenance, he is foundational to life, regardless of what people eat. Deprived of food, people starve. Deprived of Christ's presence, we become "spiritually thin." By feasting on his presence, we grow in wisdom and compassion, becoming more deeply connected to God, self and others. We are what we eat, says the cliche. Jesus, as "living bread," is the food we become.

Feed us, O Lord, with your very self that we may find eternal life.

Elizabeth-Anne Stewart

MARCH 9

May God's Vision of Me Be My Vision

**The sins of my youth and my frailties remember not;
in your kindness remember me,
because of your goodness, O Lord.** Psalm 25:7

A couple of my children are getting pretty old, which means that some memories of their childhood are more vivid than others. In fact, there are times in which one of my young adult sons will say to me, "Remember when I..." and they'll rattle off some offense they committed way back when. Nope. More often than not, I don't remember. And even if I did, it wouldn't matter much. The past is over and done with. It might impact the present, but I can't let it define it—for my sons or for myself, either. I can't let myself be burdened by guilt over sins that I committed yesterday, sins that God has forgiven and for which I've been reconciled.

I'm not going to define my children by things they did a decade ago. God doesn't define me that way, either. Isn't it time to let God's vision of me be my vision as well?

Forgiving God, release me from the chains of guilt and let me live in the present light of your love.

Amy Welborn

Lost and Found: Your Life

For whoever wishes to save his life will lose it, but whoever loses his life for my sake will save it. Luke 9:24

Lent was so much easier when we were children, wasn't it? No candy. No viewing of a favorite TV show. No fighting with a sibling or neighborhood friend.

As we get older, we grow in understanding of the awesome gift Jesus gave us in laying down his life for our redemption, and that the sacrifice we are called to make is far greater and harder than giving up sugar for six weeks. It's about putting aside the parts of ourselves, as comfortable and predictable as they may be, that keep us from God. It's about going to him, confident of forgiveness and even more confident of the joy in the new life we will live with him.

Lord, worldly temptations are seductive. Give me the courage to put them aside for you and for me.

Melanie Rigney

BE PATIENT WITH IMPERFECTION

But the LORD said to Abraham: "Why did Sarah laugh and say, 'Shall I really bear a child, old as I am?' Is anything too marvelous for the LORD to do?" Genesis 18:13-14

Sarah's laughter is understandable from a purely human perspective: the likelihood of Sarah bearing a child in her old age was near zero. But the power of God is beyond human perspectives. Sarah's barrenness was turned into fruitfulness, and that tells us what we can expect from God in our lives.

We may discover a kind of barrenness in ourselves, perhaps a deep-seated fault that prevents us from loving as fully as God desires. To be set free may seem almost impossible to us, but God can do what we cannot. In my own life, persistent prayer has freed me from some of the faults that have marred my life. Even when I've had to wait for an answer, there was an important lesson in that too. I once read somewhere that when we die, God will not ask us how perfect we have become, but rather how patient we have been with ourselves.

Lord, bring to life what is barren within me. As I try to do your will, may I be patient with myself, as you are patient with me.

Fr. Kenneth E. Grabner, C.S.C.

HALFHEARTED, TWO-FACED RESPONSES

Whatever town or village you enter, look for a worthy person in it, and stay there until you leave. Matthew 10:11

Some years ago, reflecting on Jesus' advice to his disciples to "stay there until you leave," I discovered in myself a troubling habit. I tended to accept invitations to spend time with others, all the while ready to postpone our meeting should a better offer come along. Jesus seemed to be telling the disciples and me to stick with the plan and not be lured away by more attractive propositions; to trust that God had placed me where God wanted me, even if other opportunities seemed better. The real decision depended on what I, despite my selfish habits, would offer by spending my time with that friend or acquaintance. I could be that disciple of Christ come to stay.

Resolving to kick that troublesome habit, I was soon tested. After accepting an invitation to just tag along with someone for an afternoon errand, a fellow movie lover proposed taking in the latest sleeper hit. To this day, I haven't seen the film, but I have seen the grace of the lasting friendship that began that afternoon. I'd stuck with the better offer, after all, and been blessed.

Fr. Mark Mossa, S.J.

SEEKING GOD'S HELP TO PRAY

> In the same way, the Spirit too comes to the aid of our weakness; for we do not know how to pray as we ought...
>
> Romans 8:26

With a set routine and an "orderly" life, prayer may seem relatively easy. Yes, there may be distractions along the way or the experience of "dryness" or even distaste for sitting still, but at least there is a place to pray and scheduled "quiet time." For many, however, through no choice of their own, structure and quiet are unimaginable luxuries. When one's house is full of young children or teenagers, or shared with an alcoholic spouse or parent, there is chaos. When one lives on the "party floor" of a college dorm or in a shelter for battered women, there is chaos. When one's home is a jail cell, a hospital ward or a refugee camp, there is chaos. In such conditions, even sleep is challenging, let alone quiet prayer.

A living spirituality is one we can rely on in any circumstance; it flourishes in quiet and chaos alike. Instead of relying on our own efforts, we allow the Spirit to pray in us and through us. God's grace carries us when we can barely carry ourselves.

May your breath be our prayer, O Spirit of God; breathe in us now!

Elizabeth-Anne Stewart

THE EXTRAORDINARY MERCY OF GOD

For the LORD loves his people... Psalm 149:4

You are the center of God's universe! Paul understood that more than anyone else. Those who have died and risen with Christ, those in whom the Son abides, those for whom Jesus answered to his Father with his life and with his death—they, you, are the object of God's delight. They, you, are chosen by God. Jesus spent his 33 years of life serving our needs with his own hands, wiping up our mess with his own blood, opening up our future with his own death. The life of the Word Incarnate was not a blip on the divine radar screen. All eternity God will be serving us, bent at our feet in love and mercy and compassion. God makes the impossible possible, the unbelievable reality. What is unlovable will melt in his hands like water poured from a basin. What is ostentatious will thrill to be clothed only with the brilliance of poverty. What is afraid will stand boldly with the certainty of the resurrection.

We shy away from grandeur and expectations, but we are drawn with confidence by this extraordinary mercy that will delight us for eternity.

Sr. Kathryn James Hermes, F.S.P.

MARCH 15

Recognizing Our Need to Prepare

...but the wise brought flasks of oil with their lamps.

Matthew 25:4

This parable puzzles me. Jesus seems to approve of the "wise" women who brought oil for their own lamps, but shouldn't they have shared? Did every woman really need her own lamp? This "take care of your own lamp" notion seems to contradict much of his message of sharing and generosity. In reflecting on the story, I noticed that the "foolish" seem to have waited quite a while to buy oil, though they had no lack of money. Maybe Jesus isn't critical that they forgot to bring oil, but that they didn't recognize their need and go to the merchants earlier. They didn't prepare fully.

We are like these women as we wait to meet Jesus, not knowing when he'll return. As my university chaplain often says, we're living "in the meantime" waiting for the bridegroom. It is in this long "in the meantime" when we can think that he's not coming at all that Jesus admonishes us to "stay awake." We can't let the spiritual oil of our relationship with Jesus dwindle away as the foolish women did their lamp oil.

Aileen O'Donoghue

Prayerful Shouts of Joy

Let the faithful exult in glory;
let them sing for joy upon their couches. Psalm 149:5

Whenever anyone announces, "Let us pray," whether in church, at a social event or patriotic celebration, the room gets quiet as heads are bowed and hands are folded. It is understood that God prefers solemn stillness and very serious faces. By contrast, many of the psalms, including the one we pray today, invite us to dance, play our instruments, wave the tambourine and give God joyful, vibrant words of praise.

I was once at a Papal audience with an international gathering of Benedictine women. When the Holy Father entered the room, we American and European nuns all stood at silent, stiff attention. Suddenly we were startled by shrill vocalizing from the African nuns who greeted the Pope with loud, vibrant, piercing, undulating vocal sounds—a reverent welcome from their tradition. Although we were somewhat scandalized with the unexpected outburst of noisy joy, they grasped the true biblical concept of praising with gusto. Next time you hear, "Let us pray," think of a little dance with shouts of joy.

Sr. Ruth Marlene Fox, O.S.B.

March 17

Living Faith and Faithful Living

It depends on faith... Romans 4:16

Oh, how I hear in these words the voice of my late, beloved spiritual guide, Fr. George. "It's about FAITH," he would say, capital letters and all. This sentence has worked its way into my bloodstream. Faith is what we walk on or we don't walk at all. God sustains us as we learn to trust and surrender our lives to him. I am filled with gratitude for the love, faith and guidance of Fr. George, during his life and now in a new way after his death. He taught me that we can learn to walk on faith, just as Jesus walked on water.

Teresa of Jesus suffered anguish in her faith development. A strong spiritual guide helped free her to accept her own relationship with Christ as it was, not as others thought it should be. She learned to trust her own faith and became a great reformer and spiritual leader.

Fr. George was a psychiatrist, Teresa a Doctor of the Church. Both their lives show how much we need one another if our faith lives are to thrive and mature. Our connectedness is one of the joys of following Christ in faith.

Mary Marrocco

'ST. JOSEPH, PRAY FOR ME'

When Joseph awoke, he did as the angel of the Lord had commanded him and took his wife into his home.

Matthew 1:24

At the heart of family is acceptance. Before you actually have to do it, it sounds easy. But it's not. Children are who they are, no matter what a parent's hopeful fantasies would prefer. Spouses, siblings and, yes, even parents can challenge us, as we wonder if it just wouldn't be easier to not get involved or maybe even to cut ties.

Joseph, who could have made that very choice, but allowed himself to be guided by God instead, is our model along the road to acceptance.

When I'm tempted to throw up my hands at the different choices those in my family have made, St. Joseph, pray for me.

Not only that I'm strengthened, but that I remember how someone else is accepted despite imperfection: me.

Loving God, I pray for all in my family, especially those whom I find difficult to understand.

Amy Welborn

THE FAITH OF JOB

The Lord gave and the Lord has taken away; blessed be the name of the Lord! Job 1:21

This declaration from Job surely ranks as one of the greatest professions of faith in the Bible. It is all the more astounding because it came in a period when conventional wisdom held that the loss of material possessions was a sure sign of God's disfavor. To "bless" God in the face of personal disaster was equivalent to Job praising God even as Job felt he was being cast into hell!

To be filled with praise when "God gives" is easy. We come to expect many of the "givens" of life from God—our health, our welfare and our happiness among them. We are grateful for those, although most of us probably don't thank God often enough. But to be filled with praise when "God takes away" is very difficult for us. When disaster strikes, our faith is very often too weak to continue seeing God as benevolent. When disaster strikes, we are tempted to say, "There is no God," or "God doesn't care" or "God must have it in for me."

When disaster strikes, pray for the gift of faith of Job, who held fast to the belief that what God wanted for him was good even if he couldn't understand it.

James E. Adams

A Path Toward Reconciliation

**Though your sins be like scarlet,
they may become white as snow.** Isaiah 1:18

Many have a difficulty with confession. I, too, struggled with this sacrament for years. The regular rotation of saying the same thing, hearing the same thing and reciting the same penance seemed like a divine laundry service for my soul rather than an intimate encounter with Jesus that intensified my union with him.

But in learning, searching and pleading, I have come to make my peace with confession. In preparation, I ask Jesus: "Tell me what in me most jeopardizes our relationship." I never get the same answer. It is always an unexpected and often uncomfortable revelation of a part of my life God wants to heal. It is God's revelation and activity that helps me bring into the light areas of my life that he wants to make white as snow.

Lord, I hear the eagerness of your heart to wipe away my sins. Lead me into a more mature celebration of reconciliation that I may live ever more passionately as your disciple.

Sr. Kathryn James Hermes, F.S.P.

OPEN TO HEALING

More tortuous than all else is the human heart,
   beyond remedy; who can understand it?
I, the Lord, alone probe the mind
   and test the heart... Jeremiah 17:9-10

During an ultrasound test, I was intrigued to watch on screen what the doctor was seeing inside my body while he explained it all to me. He understood much better than I and could tell what I needed. Still he, and all scientific knowledge, have barely begun to explore the mysteries of the body.

Perhaps it's similar when the heart is sick—not the physical organ, but the inner core of the person. We don't begin to understand our hearts or what ails them, except we know they suffer when they somehow part company with God. Only by letting our hearts be open to God's searching—rather than walling him out or hiding in dark corners—can they start to feel better and become better. Though we might be afraid or ashamed of inviting the Blessed One in, our Lenten devotions give us special help to be open to such healing.

Come, Lord, search my heart and know me.

Mary Marrocco

NOT HIDING IN THE DARK

But whoever lives the truth comes to the light, so that his works may be clearly seen as done in God. John 3:21

Years ago, I knew someone who was living in an apartment building that had a problem with uninvited guests—cockroaches. If you flipped on the light in the darkened kitchen, you'd just catch a glimpse of the speedy insects scattering for the still-darkened spaces under the cabinets. They were afraid of the light and felt comfortable and safe in the dark.

When we have sinned, we tend to think that denying it will make us feel better—we think we'll feel comfortable in the dark. We don't want to be reminded, don't want to go to church, don't want to acknowledge our sins. So we skitter away from the light.

Living the truth doesn't mean denying that we sin. We all sin. But when we are contrite, God's light—a warm, loving, peaceful, joyful light that penetrates our soul—awaits us. It is where we are meant to be. It is where God desires us to be.

Terence Hegarty

The Greatness of the Lord

Behold, from now on will all ages call me blessed.

Luke 1:48

Jesus called his mother "Woman." Even the saintly Francois Mauriac in his classic "Life of Jesus" (1936), remarked that such a title lacked "tenderness." But Jesus no doubt meant to honor his mother as the crown of creation, the new Eve, "mother of all the living," those now living by faith. Indeed, the tenderness would come with his dying breath, from the cross, when he gave Mary to the Beloved Disciple, and thus to all of us saying, "Behold, your mother" (John 19:27). Jesus invited "anyone who does the will of God" to identify as "my brother and my sister and my mother" (Mark 3:35). Still in the womb, he could have heard his Aunt Elizabeth call Mary "the mother of my Lord" (Luke 1:43). Praise God for women! All can say, "My soul proclaims the greatness of the Lord!" (Luke 1:46).

Miguel Dulick

FAVORED AND HUMBLE

[Mary] was greatly troubled at what was said and pondered what sort of greeting this might be. Luke 1:29

Was it the statement that she was "favored" that Mary found so troubling? Or was it that the Lord was "with" her? Apparently Gabriel's explanation was satisfying, because Mary's subsequent question is purely pragmatic, and not at all speculative: "How can this be since I have no relations with a man?"

Humility characterizes this entire exchange. In order to become human—to empty himself, as St. Paul says—God asks the help of a human being. For her part, Mary seems surprised at first to be involved at all, but then is wholly willing to accept her role in the drama that God is unfolding.

What are you and I to make of this? We celebrate today the feast of Jesus' conception in Mary's womb, the moment that the Word becomes flesh. "God became human," said St. Athanasius, "so that humans might become divine." How much more favored can you and I get? Perhaps if we understood the full meaning of that statement, we, too, would find it a bit troubling, or at the very least, humbling.

Lord, let it be done to me according to your will.

Mark Neilsen

MARCH 25

Boundless Generosity

> [Jesus] noticed a poor widow putting in two small coins.
>
> Luke 21:2

Betty is a woman in my parish who seems to know when I need a little attention. The day my husband and I brought home our new baby, she showed up with groceries and a home-cooked meal. A few months later, when my daughter's first cold was wearing us all down, Betty brought cookies and chamomile tea. And recently, when we were recovering from a death in the family, she was back again with fresh bread and daffodils. Each time, she was ready to listen if I needed to talk.

Betty is not a wealthy woman. She lives in a small house, shops in thrift stores and earns money delivering a local advertiser. Even so, she doesn't hold back when it comes to serving others. I think that this is her lived spirituality—an act of Christian engagement. And it's clear to me that all of us are called to generosity like hers and like that of the widow celebrated in Scripture.

Jesus, help me to give and not to count the cost.

Karla Manternach

Spirit-filled Worship

The holy Spirit will come upon you, and the power of the Most High will overshadow you. Luke 1:35

I've had a few "ups and downs" lately in terms of the enthusiasm and spirit that I bring to worship. A series of deaths and some tough times at work have left me weary. What I sometimes bring to Mass is, well, a bit lackluster.

The words spoken by the angel to Mary are a forceful reminder to me today that I may be relying too heavily upon my own "spirit" and not enough upon the Holy Spirit. We are called as Catholics to bring ourselves in worship so filled with the Spirit that our own lives and worries are overshadowed. The questions I ask myself today are: Do I allow the Spirit to intrude in my life? Am I willing to give up some control over my life? Can I throw myself body and soul into worship and receive the Eucharist for what it is: a spirit-filled experience that is the closest we come on earth to the glories of heaven?

That's what I want. But I can't do it alone.

Overshadow me, Holy Spirit.

Steve Givens

ACTING DESPITE MY RESERVATIONS

But she was greatly troubled at what was said and pondered what sort of greeting this might be. Luke 1:29

Mary's distress at the angel's strange greeting and her desire to know what meaning it might have for her life is certainly understandable. A call to step out of our comfort zone is not always met with enthusiasm. I vividly remember the day I first felt an interior nudge to join the parish hospital ministry. Since I am the kind of person who cannot watch a medical show on television without closing my eyes at least once, I quickly dismissed the idea as ridiculous. God seems to invite us beyond our fears. So, despite my reluctance, I eventually listened to this unexpected desire in my heart. Not only did I find the years I spent in that ministry very rewarding, the experience prepared me to walk with my mother in her final days.

Despite her reluctance, Mary stepped out in faith and gave birth to Christ. Her openness and willingness to act in spite of reservations remind me to remain open and listen carefully to the call into unknown territories.

Terri Mifek

STAYING CALM

**Let the words of my mouth and the thought of my heart
find favor before you,
O LORD, my rock and my redeemer.** Psalm 19:15

A young mother came home one day angry about something that had happened at work. Determined to hide her anger, she conversed with her five-year-old son in her usual calm and pleasant manner. But soon he asked, "Why are you angry, mom?" She replied, "What makes you think I'm angry?" He said, "You walk angry." With some effort we can control our words but it is much more difficult to control our thoughts. They frequently express themselves in body language which can speak more clearly than words. When we encounter confusing and often irritating situations, it is a challenge to keep our thoughts calm and charitable—but it is possible. With some effort, we can prayerfully practice benign thought control and retain our inner tranquility. An unruffled heart sends a peaceful message in words and actions.

Lord, bless the thoughts of our hearts and keep them calm.

Fr. James McKarns

Travel Light

[Jesus] instructed them to take nothing for the journey...

Mark 6:8

My husband taught me to travel light. I can now leave home for three days or two weeks with just one medium-sized backpack. There is a freedom that comes with less: freedom to attend to my surroundings, to the people I meet, to the local customs, foods, amusements. Instead of silly souvenirs, I buy soap or socks. Oh, I'm still tempted to take too much, but every added item becomes a burden and a potential barrier between me and someone else. If I'm worried about being robbed of my possessions, I am less welcoming of the stranger. If I'm weary of carrying too much, I have less energy for the unexpected encounter.

Most of us haul too much baggage—too much stuff, too many hard memories, too many fears. Life is a journey and Jesus instructs us to travel light—even shaking off the dust of those who are unkind to us—and to trust that what we need will be provided.

Lord Jesus, with your grace, I will let go of all that is not of you.

Paige Byrne Shortal

The Gift of the Sabbath

**If you call the sabbath a delight,
and the Lord's holy day honorable.** Isaiah 58:13

Remember when stores were closed on Sunday, and we did all our cleaning and errands on Saturday? After church on Sunday we would pile into the car and go to visit grandma or the aunts and uncles, or they would come to us. Mom usually made a baked chicken with mashed potatoes and green beans. While the grown-ups relaxed, we girls did the dishes, but kept a keen ear open to the women's conversations. This is how we learned about being wives and mothers.

When my own children were growing up there was always an outing of some sort after church, often a picnic or trip to a zoo or museum.

Isaiah gives us strong injunctions to keep the sabbath and promises us that if we do, we shall know delight! Sabbath is for us. It is a divine gift meant to nurture and sustain us. Let us receive this gift gratefully and use it wisely to honor our Lord!

Lord, I will delight in the sabbath, your holy day!

Jennifer Christ

March 31

Spring of Love

> **Jesus, tired from his journey, sat down there at the well...
> about noon. A woman of Samaria came to draw water. Jesus
> said to her, "Give me a drink."** John 4:6-7

Samaritan women were considered by Jews to be ritually unclean;
therefore, Jewish men were expressly forbidden to take food or
drink from them. Jesus pays no attention to this. As soon as this
Samaritan woman comes to the well, he asks her for a drink. She,
not only Samaritan but shunned by her own community, was
stunned. When she questions him, he tells her of the living water
he has to give her: "whoever drinks the water I shall give will never
thirst; ...a spring of water welling up to eternal life" (John 4:14).

It is a continuing source of wonder to me that God comes right
to us, meets us in the middle of our challenging lives, paying no
attention to our imperfections, actually thirsting for our response,
wanting to give us the living water of love.

*Beloved God, what a blessing to drink from the spring of your love
welling up to eternal life.*

Patricia Livingston

BEAUTY IN THE DESERT

**So I will allure her;
I will lead her into the desert
and speak to her heart.** Hosea 2:16

God leads us into the wilderness of ourselves—to be transformed and able to meet others in the heart.

St. Mary of Egypt taught this to a hermit/monk named Zosimus (St. Zosimus of Palestine) who thought nobody could teach him about holiness. He thought that he knew it all. God led him into the desert. There he met the "nobody" Mary, ragged and alone. He loved her instantly and begged for her story.

She told of her wild youth, seducing men, following her fancy. One day, following the men into the Church of the Holy Sepulcher, she found her way barred. She realized how lost and alone she was and wept. The Mother of God comforted her and led her into church, then into the desert where, for 47 years, she worked out her inner thirsts. Zosimus saw her humility, beauty and strength. Changed by their encounter, he told her story to others who wrote it down soon after. He said her tears made the desert flowers bloom.

St. Mary, teach us to see beauty in the desert places of ourselves.

Mary Marrocco

APRIL 2

The Power of Small Kindnesses

Mary took a liter of costly perfumed oil made from genuine aromatic nard and anointed the feet of Jesus and dried them with her hair; the house was filled with the fragrance of the oil. John 12:3

Perhaps you have a child with leukemia, or a parent with Alzheimer's disease, or a spouse with a drug addiction. If so, you know the pain of seeing a loved one suffer and the feeling of powerlessness.

While it's unlikely any of us will come up with a surefire cure for our loved ones' illnesses, we can do what Mary of Bethany did for Jesus. We can provide a respite through a special treat such as a foot rub. We can read aloud from a favorite book. We can pray together. We can listen when the person shares his or her pains and fears. And while none of these small actions may change the eventual outcome, they can ease the transition and bring us all closer to Christ.

Jesus, grant me the patience to offer kindnesses in your name and the grace to accept them when they are offered to me.

Melanie Rigney

WHAT I HAVE, I GIVE

I have neither silver nor gold, but what I do have I give you...

Acts 3:6

I was introduced to this verse of Scripture as the title of the first collection of music recorded by the St. Louis Jesuits—*Neither Silver Nor Gold*. I was an adult convert and had never met Jesuits, or any other religious men and women, until my mid-20s. I was astonished that they tried to live like the Utopians I had studied in college—sharing what they had, taking only what they needed. This was also the ideal of the early Church, the goal of the first Christians.

Why? What was it about Jesus and his teaching that inspires people to attempt this way of life? Love one another. Whoever wants to be first, be the last. Give away your extra cloak to someone who has none. As I do, so must you do.

It works. The happiest, most peaceful, most blessed people I know are those who live with open hearts and hands and homes to those on their path; with open eyes to the possibilities of making this world a better place.

Paige Byrne Shortal

APRIL 4

Letting Go, Letting God

If this endeavor or this activity is of human origin, it will destroy itself. But if it comes from God, you will not be able to destroy them; you may even find yourselves fighting against God. Acts 5:38-39

My softball team was enjoying an evening of barbecue, backyard volleyball and fellowship. On my way out, my teammate asked if he could call or have dinner with me. Attracted but not yet ready to enter a relationship, I turned him down. But we kept in touch as friends, and a few months later, I decided to ask him out after Sunday Mass. This time *he* turned *me* down—he was dating someone else at the time.

This was confusing: Was God opening my heart to this man, or were my feelings simply of human origin? Was I fighting against God? I tried to move on, but a week later, I received a phone call. My friend was again available, and he wanted to see me. This time I didn't let the invitation pass me by. We were married two years later.

Open my heart to your promptings, God.

Julia DiSalvo

WITH GOD AT OUR CENTER

Moreover, God is able to make every grace abundant for you, so that in all things, always having all you need, you may have an abundance for every good work. 2 Corinthians 9:8

What is it about shopping, stuff, desire and anxiety?

Shopping for toys or pretty things may not be my particular weakness, but something else is. I guess you would call it lifestyle shopping. I am forever thinking that if the space I live in would more closely resemble the showrooms at, say, Pottery Barn or Ikea, I could get more done, and life, in general, would be more what it should be. I imagine myself in those spaces, and it just seems as if everything would be so much easier there.

Well, Paul tells me something different about all of this. Put the catalogs away, for not a dime needs to be spent or a single faux-industrial table arranged. That dwelling space with God at the center is sufficient, not just for survival, but for so much more.

Loving God, I open myself to your abundant grace today.

Amy Welborn

Two Daughters

Courage, daughter! Matthew 9:22

I imagine Matthew 9:18-26 as a play. Act 1: Jesus is approached by Jairus, a synagogue official, who humbles himself before this itinerant healer to beg for the life of his daughter. Act 2: On the way to Jairus's house, Jesus is waylaid by a woman who seeks relief from constant bleeding. As he comforts her, whom he calls "daughter"—the only time in the Scriptures Jesus uses this title—a servant comes running to say that Jairus' daughter has died. Act 3: Jesus insists that they continue to Jairus' house. As they walk along, I imagine a conversation. A grieving and bitter Jairus grumbles that if Jesus hadn't wasted time with that unclean woman who could not even enter his synagogue, perhaps they would have reached his daughter in time. Jesus gently explains that every woman is a daughter; that during the twelve years Jairus' daughter has lived a healthy, happy life, this other daughter has suffered—a suffering made worse by contempt and isolation. The act ends with Jesus at the home of Jairus, lovingly raising up the little girl.

Paige Byrne Shortal

HUNGRY? GOD DELIVERS

Where can I get meat to give to all this people?... I cannot carry all this people by myself, for they are too heavy for me.
Numbers 11:13-14

Mealtime can be a source of enjoyment or stress for me, depending on the circumstances. When the kids are occupied and the recipe and ingredients are on hand, I get great satisfaction from preparing dinners and setting them on the table. But when I fail to plan ahead and am faced with the prospect of a crabby family and/or an expensive night out, anxiety enters and threatens to take over.

If, like Moses, I turn to God in these moments, I remember that he has and will continue to provide. Either directly or through my husband, God steps in and helps open my eyes to the abundance before me. Somehow we are fed and filled—and blessed to appreciate his gifts and rely on them.

God, teach us to trust through gratitude and generosity.

Julia DiSalvo

A Healing Time for Us All

Those who are well do not need a physician, but the sick do.

Matthew 9:12

I took my young children to Lourdes. While there, they were struck—as nearly anyone would be—by the presence of the sick. It is not just that the sick are present. It's that they are given pride of place. In any procession, any prayer service, the wheelchairs are first.

The children asked why, and so we talked not only about Lourdes and healing, but also about what Jesus says about the last—in the world's eyes—being first in the Kingdom. About what Christ tells us about meeting him in the suffering.

But there's this too: It seems to me that the predominance given to the sick at Lourdes is a visible sign of the internal reality of every pilgrim, whether they can walk or not. They're a sign to remind us that we are all "the sick." We've all come to Christ through Mary in this place because, without him, we are not well, not fine, not whole. Why would we be on the journey if we were?

Jesus, I come to you in weakness, trusting in your healing power.

Amy Welborn

A SPIRIT OF BELIEF

> **The Lord said to her in reply, "Martha, Martha, you are anxious and worried about many things. There is need of only one thing. Mary has chosen the better part and it will not be taken from her."** Luke 10:41-42

On a regular basis, I feel like Mary and Martha are waging a war within me to see who will gain control. The Martha in me worries too much, scrambles to do too much and lives by a to-do list. If I let Martha take over, I'm far too busy doing and not busy being.

The Mary in me makes time to see beyond myself. Mary makes time for God. Mary really listens to people. Mary prays before responding, rather than simply reacting.

The Martha in me strives, but it's never enough; the Mary in me knows that I am already enough. Martha goes at breakneck speed but can't fit it all in. Mary goes at grace pace, and the most important things are done well.

It's hard to be more like Mary in a Martha-oriented world. Just for today, let's try to exchange a spirit of busy for a spirit of belief.

Kristin Armstrong

Impelled by Love

When he was in Bethany reclining at table in the house of Simon the leper, a woman came with an alabaster jar of perfumed oil, costly genuine spikenard. She broke the alabaster jar and poured it on his head. Mark 14:3

We can almost hear this woman's nervous intake of breath, her wildly beating heart, as she summoned her courage and entered, uninvited, the exclusive gathering of men in the house of Simon the leper. Did she hesitate when she felt their shocked glance in her direction, their silent disapproval of her boldness? Did she tremble as they moved from stunned silence to angry criticism of her appearance and her action? I imagine that none of those elements stood in her way. This woman saw no one but Jesus, and she was impelled to offer this loving, extravagant gesture. The fragrance remains, and the story is forever remembered and celebrated.

Sr. Chris Koellhoffer, I.H.M.

Lost and Found

Or what woman having ten coins and losing one would not light a lamp and sweep the house, searching carefully until she finds it? Luke 15:8

Few things are as annoying as misplacing something that we need, and often need right now—our glasses, the car keys, one sock, a document we put somewhere for safekeeping. Add to this list from your own experience. Depending on how important or how critical the lost item is, we often devote significant time to searching for it, retracing our steps, culling through our memory for our last remembrance of the disappeared object.

This parable of the lost coin companions the lost sheep and the lost child in a series of stories we might call "the lost and found." In this parable, the woman stands in for Jesus, never giving up on us, searching with care, urgency and longing for our return to his unending love.

Sr. Chris Koellhoffer, I.H.M.

The Miracle of Life

He is not God of the dead, but of the living... Luke 20:38

God gives, gives and gives *life*. It's life so pure, so powerful, that death itself couldn't hold Christ in the grave: He burst the lock of the tomb. Sometimes it seems our whole Christian existence is intended simply to teach our every molecule that life, not death, is the victor.

We need help in learning this because death's power seems total, its victory inexorable. When we buried a young man who was so full of life, it seemed impossible we should be standing by his grave. How could we stand there and still claim the God of the living? How could we not, if we belonged to Christ?

In Maccabees, a mother and seven sons have faith so strong it takes them beyond the grave. We need their witness, and each other's. He is God of the living, and his Church is a living testimony that God is Lord. In surrendering our lives to him—and the lives of those we love so dearly—we receive life that never fades.

Lord, where there is death, work your miracle of life.

Mary Marrocco

The Unknown Power of Faith

Daughter, your faith has saved you. Mark 5:34

In this quote, I find myself thinking about what Jesus did not say. He doesn't say that he, or God, had saved her because of her faith. He says her faith saved her.

Nonbelievers and those struggling with doubt have been heard to ask, "If God exists, why doesn't God make that fact obvious?" This statement from Jesus may hint at part of the answer. Perhaps there is something profoundly important in faith itself, separate from God's other gifts. Perhaps in the sometimes frustrating, painful unknowing when we act out of faith, not sure at all that we actually believe, some change is wrought in us, some hardness softened that simply can't be softened any other way. In those times when my doubt is strong and I feel that I'm "just going through the motions," I try to keep this in mind as I pray for the faith I need to keep up the motions.

Dear Lord, thank you for the gift of faith.

Aileen O'Donoghue

Being Christ to One Another

She came and fell at his feet. Mark 7:25

The Canaanite woman could easily exemplify many of us hanging onto life by its edges. A Gentile, this mother must have suspected that she'd risk ridicule as she thrust her way through a crowd of predominantly male Jewish onlookers to fling herself at the feet of Jesus. Desperation frequently leaves one with few options.

If we allow others to stand between us and God, we allow ourselves to be marginalized. Mention "a marginal existence" and many immediately think of the homeless. But the litany of the marginalized includes migrant workers, the elderly struggling to make ends meet or prisoners being tortured. Those who've trained their eyes to shy away from another's plight may in their own way be marginalized.

If we desire to be as Christ to one another, then we must strive to view the world through his eyes. Perhaps as important, we need to graciously accept the offerings of those who would act as Christ to us.

Phillis Harris-Brooks

WEEPING CLOSE TO HOME

You have not spoken rightly concerning me, as has my servant Job. Job 42:7

Of all Job's afflictions, the least tolerable was the "comfort" of his friends! Even God rebukes them for their busybodying. So, Jesus had to tell the "Daughters of Jerusalem," on the way to the cross, "do not weep for me; weep instead for yourselves and for your children" (Luke 23:28). Women had nursed his ministry ever since Galilee, and Jesus was surely grateful, but now reality was upon them. As hard as it was to imagine at that moment—"when the wood is green," as Jesus puts it—things were going to get worse— "when it is dry" (Luke 23:31). I wonder if Mary overheard these dire words; she was already weeping for her child! As predicted by Simeon, the sword was piercing Mary's soul! Could she possibly have seen future woes, when her newfound children, the disciples, would be sacrificed and scattered in her son's name? There are no rules for weeping. Just keep it close to home.

Miguel Dulick

GATHER TO EAT

So whether you eat or drink...do everything for the glory of God. 1 Corinthians 10:31

I don't usually think of myself as eating and drinking for the glory of God! I'm afraid I mostly think of my own taste buds, waistline or need of nourishment. Paul speaks of how our smallest actions witness to others, urging the Corinthians not to act in ways that might hurt others' faith. Pointing to food, he highlights one of the most crucial places where our faith might be expressed. Eating and drinking is what we do together; it's how we socialize. I think of the thirty-pound turkey my sister-in-law raised herself, then served at a Thanksgiving dinner for twenty-five people. The gathering happened around the food. The gift in her preparing that banquet was part of the richness. I've also visited homes with no dinner table, since people eat fast food or in front of the TV. Food becomes an individual exercise.

If a shared meal is difficult or impossible at home, we can still partake in our Lord's banquet. Eucharist is his invitation to the shared meal with him and with one another. And it's an experience we should not miss.

Mary Marrocco

Finding Perspective

**Take delight in the Lord,
  and he will grant you your heart's requests.** Psalm 37:4

Our culture tells us to revere our desires and pursue them with drive and determination. This philosophy has so shaped our manner of living that many of us are exhausted and left empty. With each new achievement or acquisition, we are left with smaller and shorter lived moments of satisfaction before pushing on to the next pursuit. After a time, we cease to even recognize what was our heart's desire when we began.

We are living lives with less peace and less fulfillment. Our relationships, our careers, our very souls have paid a high price. If we are lucky, we reach a critical moment in life, culminating in a choice between following God and following our whims.

When we pursue God, knowledge of him and relationship with him, all other things fall sweetly into place. He never forgets the desires of our heart; after all, he put them there in the first place. When our delight is in him, circumstances fade to their proper position—the background.

Kristin Armstrong

WAIT TRAINING

After patient waiting, he obtained the promise. Hebrews 6:15

My seven-year-old Border collie is not very patient. If he wants to play catch, he'll place a toy right on your lap. If you raise it to be thrown, beware—those who delay may be hit with sixty-five pounds of muscle, fur and paw!

I am impatient too. I have my desires, my dreams and expectations. I am frustrated by others who don't meet my needs and often resort to taking what I want. I know I've hurt others in the process, but I just can't seem to wait.

What can I do? When my dog approaches to play, I tell him to sit. Though his focus is still on the toy, he obeys and waits for the throw. Perhaps I should train myself to sit when I'm impatient too. If I wait and listen to the voice of the one who cares for me, I may get even more than I asked for.

Father, wait for me, even though I don't always wait for you.

Julia DiSalvo

Passing on the Faith

> I recall your sincere faith that first lived in your grandmother Lois and in your mother Eunice and that I am confident lives also in you. 2 Timothy 1:5

When I was a child, my grandmother lived with us, a live-in baby-sitter on those nights when my parents went out. For me, those were nights of playing rummy, eating popcorn and, as the evening grew old, a time for singing. She taught me songs of faith that fed my young interest in both music and church. She wasn't a great singer, but she closed her eyes and sang with meaning and passion that inspired me and set me on the road toward my love of God and sacred music.

As we reflect on our spiritual lives and the decisions we have made to follow Christ, we often recall, perhaps, moving and meaningful times we have spent in private and communal prayer. We think of deep conversations with spiritual guides and good friends. We treasure sacramental moments. But do we remember the simple and sincere lessons of faith given as divine gifts of the Father through an obedient parent or grandparent—lessons that give us spiritual confidence many years down the road?

God, thank you for those who pass on the faith.

Steve Givens

Trust in God

**Take delight in the Lord,
and he will grant you your heart's requests.** Psalm 37:4

I wish I had this psalm printed in fortune cookies for all the friends and students who have told me that all they want is "to be in a relationship." At times in our lives, all of us have felt that dull ache of pain that loneliness brings. What if that ache were actually a gentle reminder sent from God to draw us into a deeper relationship with him and to nurture a loving relationship with ourselves?

Recently, I heard a man say that he decided to trust that God had someone in mind for him to be his life's partner. He just didn't know who that person was. So, on those days when he felt most lonely, he wrote love letters to his future spouse. On New Year's Eve when he had no one to kiss, on Valentine's Day when he had no one to send him a card, he wrote love letters to "his heart's desire" and trusted that God would open his heart and his eyes to the right person. On his wedding day, his gift to his bride was a box of love letters written to her when he didn't even know who she was.

Claire J. King

With a Little Help From Friends

We must consider how to rouse one another to love and good works. Hebrews 10:24

Looking back on my life and the many good and true friendships I have had, I realize that the very best and lasting relationships have been with those individuals who have shared my own beliefs in Christ and the power of faith. They have not been bystanders and onlookers to my spiritual life; rather, they have played crucial roles in it. They have been willing and brave enough to encourage me to a life filled with love and good works by their words and their actions. I hope that I have been able to do the same for them.

For as much as some people want to see their faith lives as "personal and private," Christ calls us to no such thing. He calls us to a communal Christianity in which we worship, celebrate and grieve together. We are not called into competition with one another for the best seat at the banquet and a seat at Jesus' right hand, but instead to friendships filled with encouragement, mutual love and shared moments of charity. He calls us to be the Church.

Thank you, Jesus, for friends who urge me on toward you.

Steve Givens

April 22

In Time, God Hears Us

In distress you called, and I rescued you;
    Unseen, I answered you in thunder. Psalm 81:8

When I was younger, the rumbling of thunder would send me into a panic, but somehow over the years, my prayers were answered and the fear dissolved without my even realizing how or when it happened. It seems our life of faith is often like that; we yell, God responds and eventually we recognize the wonder of what has taken place.

As I look back over the years, and there are more years to look back on than I would like to admit, a pattern emerges. Things I counted on disappeared; children grew up and moved out; through death and unforeseen circumstances, relationships and work opportunities I cherished ended. I protested, sometimes very loudly, but eventually I become aware that the very things I resisted thrust me into new depths of prayer, new images of God and hopefully new levels of compassion and understanding—all things I have ardently prayed for through the years.

Terri Mifek

WHAT ARE OUR EASTER EXPERIENCES?

So the other disciples said to him, "We have seen the Lord."

John 20:25

A friend told me recently how her prayer life had shifted from being "God-centered" to "Christ-centered." She explained how each time she prayed, she began to feel a tangible sense of Christ's presence. It was as though Jesus had broken through the doors of my friend's consciousness and she was being encouraged to focus on Jesus and Jesus alone. She also experienced the call to participate more deeply in his life and to let him become the source of her whole life.

Where do we see the Lord? Whose are the faces in which we see his face reflected? In what ways do we encounter Jesus in our daily lives? These questions invite us to reflect on the Easter experience as it is happening now. It is not enough to catch the spirit of wonder and enthusiasm recorded in the gospels. The disciples' experiences of the risen Jesus were their own experiences. We need to be in touch with our own encounters with the risen Christ. As my friend has discovered, Jesus is just as accessible in our time as he was in the days immediately following his resurrection.

Elizabeth-Anne Vanek

APRIL 24

Rock-solid Faith

I love you, O Lord, my strength,
O Lord, my rock... Psalm 18:2

I enjoy collecting rocks—all sizes, all shapes. Our motherhouse is in Wisconsin in what was once Native American territory. I once found a bulky, yellow-tinted rock with a curious shape. I have kept it as a paper weight, and it reminds me of some of my origins near the Mississippi River in Wisconsin.

Another experience, however, is the one that most reminds me of the strength of rock. My father used to take us children to the shore of Lake Michigan on a late winter or early spring afternoon. We walked around a point of land that juts out into the lake. As a small child, I had the feeling that I was surrounded by water, wind and sky. The wind would lash at the rocks on which we stood. The waves seemed huge and sprayed us with cold darts of water. Somehow I wasn't afraid because the rocks seemed so solid.

I can pray as the psalmist, "I love you, O Lord, my strength, O Lord, my rock," because I, too, have experienced God as a solid presence in joy and in sorrow, always there to support me.

Sr. Marguerite Zralek, O. P.

QUESTIONS FOR LIFE

Jesus said to her, "Woman, why are you weeping? Whom are you looking for?" She thought it was the gardener and said to him, "Sir, if you carried him away, tell me where you laid him, and I will take him." John 20:15

The two questions Jesus asks in the garden that Sunday morning speak of both loss and desire. "Why are you weeping?" Jesus asks a grieving Mary, and Jesus asks us. We weep for many reasons, for what has been taken from us, for what has been shattered, fractured, disappeared, for what is beyond fixing, beyond repairing, beyond restoring. We weep for relationships broken, lives ended, dreams unfulfilled.

The second question digs deeper. "Whom are you looking for?" Not *what,* but *whom.* Here our words are inadequate to satisfactorily define or describe. But we intuit that the answer is as near as the desire of our beating hearts—we long for you, the risen One, the Holy One. Today. Always.

Sr. Chris Koellhoffer, I.H.M.

JESUS, NOT IGNORANCE, IS BLISS

The God of Abraham, the God of Isaac, and the God of Jacob, the God of our ancestors, has glorified his servant Jesus... Acts 3:13

The people in Jesus' time were amazed by the healings that were occurring around them. They attributed the miraculous works to Peter and John, not recognizing that the healing power came from Jesus. "You acted out of ignorance," they are told.

As Christians, we cannot claim such ignorance. We know much more about Jesus and his divine nature.

But before we feel superior to the contemporaries of the apostles, we could ask ourselves how often we have failed to recognize Jesus in others. Every day, in both dramatic and seemingly mundane fashion, miracles still occur, souls are still saved. Through Christ may we understand that we serve as modern-day apostles, bringing this knowledge of who Jesus really is to all whom we encounter.

Jesus, my Savior, help me listen to you; fill my mind and heart with your knowledge and peace.

Terence Hegarty

'I Am Home for God'

> And all shall sing, in their festive dance:
> **"My home is within you."** Psalm 87:7

After feeling lost at prayer for days in a row, one day I will wake up feeling at home. I visit a school or a place of business, and the moment I step in the door, I feel at home. I shop at one store in preference to another because the first has more of a homey feeling. Home connotes welcome, tranquility, security, rest.

Jesus, too, had this sense of home. He seemed at home when he washed his disciples' feet, when he was in Martha and Mary's house, when he fed the 5,000, when he cured the blind and the lame. Home was where he could be true to who he was, where Abba and he could be one.

The above psalm has a startling line: "My home is within you." It is one thing for me to say I feel at home in the Father. It is quite another to realize that the Father finds a home in me! Living the implications of that statement will get me through anything today. And should something loom its ugly head at me, making me feel out of sorts or less of a person than I am, may I remember that I am home for God. Can anything really be more important than that?

Sr. Charleen Hug, S.N.D.

Companion

> ...while he was with them at table, he took bread, said the
> blessing, broke it, and gave it to them. With that their eyes
> were opened and they recognized him, but he vanished from
> their sight. Luke 24:30-31

My grandmother would bake so much bread that I'd spend all
morning delivering the loaves to neighbors. Later, she'd sit on the
porch talking to everyone who passed by. My grandmother knew
the names of all the children, the concerns of all their parents and
the needs of all her neighbors. She'd rest her prayer book on her
lap and listen to those who climbed up on the porch to sit with
her. Before they left, my grandmother promised to pray for them.

On the road to Emmaus, the disciples welcome a companion
to walk with them. The word companion comes from the Latin
words meaning *with* and *bread*. Later, Jesus reveals himself to them
in the breaking of the bread. Thanks to my grandmother, I have
come to recognize Jesus in the kindness of others, and I look for
ways to be a companion to those in need.

Deborah Meister

A PRAYER OF AWARENESS

If you bring your gift to the altar, and there recall that your brother has anything against you, leave your gift there at the altar, go first and be reconciled... Matthew 5:23-24

We would rather not think about whether someone is upset with us or has hurt feelings because of something we said or did. We would rather not know that our relationship with God is connected to our other relationships. We would rather not think about whether people across town, or on the other side of the world, might have a legitimate grievance against us, people who are poor and hungry in part because of choices our society has made.

We can make choices that change the way we live our individual lives, and that can be good and helpful. But even when we do what we can, it may not make a big difference to the poor of the world. It makes a difference, however, if we choose to remain aware, if we don't pretend things are not the way they are. That can be a good, ongoing prayer.

Lord Jesus, help me to be aware of my relationship with all of humankind.

Mitch Finley

APRIL 30

We Are Earthen Vessels

We hold this treasure in earthen vessels, that the surpassing power may be of God and not from us. 2 Corinthians 4:7

Occasionally I watch *Antiques Roadshow* on TV. Often people bring for appraisal items such as a vase, a teapot or a set of dishes. Sometimes these items are worth thousands of dollars. Other times, their value is depreciated by subtle cracks, broken handles or chipped paint. But whatever their condition, the fact remains: these vases, teapots and dishes have survived, despite their fragility. Their survival is all the more amazing since some of them were used on a regular basis for decades, or they sat neglected for years in dry attics or damp basements or they withstood rough transport across vast lands or oceans.

St. Paul tells us we are all earthen vessels. What an appropriate image! Though vulnerable, we are still valuable. Though imperfect, we are precious. Though flawed, we are cherished. Our survival ultimately comes not from our own power, but from the surpassing power of God.

Loving Potter, help me be more patient with the chips, cracks and flaws in myself and in others.

Sr. Melannie Svoboda, S.N.D.

A HEALING WORD FROM JESUS

Jesus said to her, "Mary!" She turned and said to him in Hebrew, "Rabbouni," which means Teacher. John 20:16

The triumphant and glorious story of the resurrection begins in John's Gospel with a scene noteworthy for its poignant simplicity. There is a woman mourner, an unknown gardener and then the single word, "Mary!" In hearing Jesus' voice speak her name, Mary of Magdala was catapulted into a new reality where anything is possible and death is not the ultimate victor. One word took all the pain from her heart. One word reconnected her to what she thought she had lost: hope, love and purpose. Her life changed, never to be the same again. How simple, yet how extraordinary!

When we think of the resurrection, it is good to remember that, without fanfare or grandiosity, Jesus reentered the world in a personal and private encounter with a single disciple by calling her name. Jesus seeks each of us, individually, at those moments when we are most likely to recognize the voice that names us with a word gentle and intimate, yet life-changing and death-shattering.

Lord, may we make ourselves ready to hear your loving call to life.

Nancy F. Summers

Christ-like in Small Things

> **Whoever wishes to be great among you shall be your servant; whoever wishes to be first among you shall be your slave.**
>
> Matthew 20:26-27

My parents came here for a visit to help with the kids during an unusually busy time. All the while they were here, they were looking for more to do. They glued kitchen chairs that kept coming apart. They fixed a hinge so a door would close properly. They organized a closet, replaced batteries and washed countless dishes.

Time with my parents often leaves me marveling at their generosity. It also makes me want to be more generous myself. Sometimes I get so caught up in taking care of my family and myself that I do little for others. I mean, who needs any more to do? Yet Jesus calls us to serve others, and not just those we love.

I don't have to create a foundation or run a nonprofit to be of service. Like Mother Teresa said, I can do small things with great love. I can bake bread for a neighbor, hold a door for a stranger and stop cutting people off when I drive.

Jesus, help me look for ways to serve others.

Karla Manternach

WITH ALL YOUR HEART ...

Therefore, you shall love the LORD, your God, with all your heart, and with all your soul, and with all your strength.

Deuteronomy 6:5

Sometimes we don't give it our all. We nod without really listening when our spouse wants to go over vacation plans yet again. We fail to take our usual care with an assignment at work, figuring what we've done is "good enough." We make a mental grocery list instead of truly listening and reflecting during the homily. It's not that we've done anything disruptive or evil; we're just not totally there.

But half-heartedness doesn't work with God. He calls on us to show our love with every thought, word and action, not just when we want or need something. God wants our fully engaged presence all the time. He desires nothing less than our whole heart—because that's what he gives us every day in every way.

Lord, I humbly ask that you help me show my love for you at all times.

Melanie Rigney

CALLED TO GIVE

Whoever sows sparingly will also reap sparingly...

2 Corinthians 9:6

I have been blessed with the examples of generosity of those around me. A friend who lives simply uses her income on mission work. A couple offers their guest house as a place for groups to meet. Another friend hands me the key to her rural home so I can write close to nature.

Yet I often hesitate before I give. Can I afford it? Especially when times are uncertain, it's natural to ask. God's word reminds us of reward beyond our present circumstances. And sometimes we see a small example of that here on earth.

I recently looked at some lotion I had just purchased and realized a friend would enjoy it. I hesitated, knowing my dry skin would itch without some sort of balm. But I prepared a gift bag for my friend anyway. The next day, I received a gift certificate—to a store that specializes in skin care products!

Today, it might only be lotion, but when we remember we are called to give, we surely will discover the even greater reward that awaits us.

Beth Dotson Brown

Love Is Inclusive

Casting herself prostrate upon the ground, she said to him, "Why should I, a foreigner, be favored with your notice?"

Ruth 2:10

I was in South Korea with a group of Sisters visiting a historic site when a group of kindergartners walked by with their teachers. Several children pointed at us and said something. When I asked a Korean Sister what they had said, she replied, "Foreigners!" I thought: We learn quite young who is one of us and who is not.

Ruth is amazed by Boaz's kindness toward her, a foreigner. As a Moabite, she was shunned by many in Bethlehem, yet Boaz welcomes her and eventually even marries her. Amazingly, Ruth the foreigner becomes a direct ancestor of King David and, many years later, Jesus the Messiah.

Whom do we label as foreigner? Whom do we exclude from our welcoming? The sobering reality is this: In denying certain individuals our love, we may be hindering God's beautiful designs.

God of Inclusiveness, help me to welcome others into my life, even those I may think of as foreigners.

Sr. Melannie Svoboda, S.N.D.

Mercy, Not Fairness

Are you envious because I am generous? Matthew 20:15

Oh, those vineyard workers. Can we really blame those who had been working since dawn—*dawn,* I tell you—for being upset about receiving the same wage as those who didn't go to work until late in the afternoon? It just wasn't fair!

That's the thing about God. He isn't fair. But he is merciful. And we should all feel exceedingly grateful and blessed for that. His love and generosity is available to all of us, whether we come to him as infants at baptism or as adult converts. He desires to draw us in when we've been away for an hour, a month or decades. He delights in us and finds joy in showing his grace upon us, regardless of the time of day that we enter his vineyard. May we celebrate, not be envious, when we see how he welcomes our brothers and sisters who get there a little late.

Father, I am humbled by your mercy.

Melanie Rigney

Full Members, Part of the Plan

[God] has now reconciled...you... Colossians 1:22

The other night I realized something about myself: I tend to make everything into a project, and, true to form, that includes my relationship with God. That may seem to be a good thing, to be intent on growing in relationship with God. And it is true that our growing friendship with God hinges in part on our interest, love and presence. But I often forget that Jesus accomplished something that established my status in this relationship. Before we were even born, humanity was reconciled to God, and through baptism, we got the full package deal.

We are members of the "family"—paid in full, premium membership. We are children of God, and Jesus is bound and determined to present us to his Father, holy and irreproachable at the end. No matter what we've done in life or what's been done to us, Jesus' plan for us remains.

Paul knew this—for God had sought him out and dramatically changed the direction of his life. It is this life-changing God about whom Paul preaches—our hope and our salvation!

Sr. Kathryn James Hermes, F.S.P.

MAY 8

Expanding Our Hearts

My mother and my brothers are those who hear the word of God and act on it. Luke 8:21

For many of us, particularly those with a strong devotion to Mary, this statement is almost unbearably harsh. How could Jesus reject his mother this way? But what he says reflects, I think, what is true of most of our relationships with family. They usually don't "get" us the way our friends or colleagues who understand our motives and our stresses do. My own mantra about families is that God gives them to us so we learn how to spend a lifetime loving people we wouldn't necessarily choose as friends.

So Jesus' words, rather than offending us, can give us comfort that the periodic alienation we feel from our families is something he has experienced and understands. We are not alone in the lifelong challenge of loving those who share our origins and our biology, but grow and change in ways that mystify us as much as we mystify them. Let us call on him in our difficult moments to expand our hearts to love what we can't comprehend in our families.

Aileen O'Donoghue

The Teacher Is Always With Us

She thought it was the gardener and said to him, "Sir, if you carried him away, tell me where you laid him, and I will take him." Jesus said to her, "Mary!" She turned and said to him in Hebrew, "Rabbouni," which means Teacher. John 20:15-16

There is such a sweetness to John's account of Mary Magdalene visiting the tomb. While all four gospels relate a story of discovering the empty tomb, and Mary is in them all, in John's Gospel, she converses with the risen Jesus. When she meets him in the garden outside the tomb, she assumes he's a gardener. But when he says her name, she responds immediately, "Teacher." I always imagined her response with an exclamation point—that she shouted out, *"Yay, Teacher, it's you! You're back!"* But on closer reading, I realize it says something else—she turns to him and says, "Teacher." It's a respectful, relief-filled statement. *Here is my teacher. All is well again.* I read it now as consolation, not celebration.

Teacher, when I am in despair or suffering with anxiety, let me hear you say my name and remember that you are always with me.

Phil Fox Rose

MY MOTHER TAUGHT ME

...those who obey the LORD honor their mother. Sirach 3:6

My mother taught me to look both ways before crossing the street. She taught me that elbows don't belong on the dinner table. She taught me that sarcasm should be employed to illicit joy, not hurt.

My mother taught me that common sense isn't very common, that hard work isn't a burden, that my guardian angel was real, but that I still shouldn't ride my skateboard into traffic.

My mother taught me that God loves me even more than she did. My mother, her mother and my father all taught me the virtues of the Catholic faith.

My mother taught me that if you're faced with a terminal illness in your 50s, you can still laugh. As she neared death at age 61, my mother taught me that you can be brave, tough, loving and faithful in the face of it.

My mother taught me to obey the Lord and live a life of faith.

Thanks, Mom.

Terence Hegarty

HOPE'S LANDING PAD

**My strength and my courage is the LORD,
and he has been my savior.** Psalm 118:14

When I was a patient in a big Catholic hospital recently, my room looked out on a helicopter landing pad. At night, it sparkled with lights. When the helicopter came in, I tried to get to the window to see it. The pad was not meant to be shaped like a cross, but it looked like one. It became a symbol of hope for me every night. Years ago, when I worked as a chaplain at another hospital, I also watched the helicopter come in from the view of helping others, of having hope for my patients. Now I was watching it for myself, and my eyes filled with tears.

Symbols of hope during the Easter season are important. In Church we look at the symbols of Easter, such as lilies, incense, the Paschal candle, the Alleluia and, of course, the reality of the Risen Life of Christ hidden in the Eucharist. In our homes, we look at symbols of hope in our crucifixes, in holy water. We look in each other's eyes too. At times, we need every symbol we can hang on to, including helicopter pads, to remind us that Christ has risen. Alleluia!

Sr. Marguerite Zralek, O. P.

Mothering the Masses

When Jesus saw his mother and the disciple there whom he loved, he said to his mother, "Woman, behold, your son."

John 19:26

She was all he had left on earth. They had taken his clothing, his tunic, his health and, as far as they were concerned, his dignity. Jesus sacrificed all of it without complaint. But he waited until just before the end to offer up his relationship with his beloved mother. Now we would all belong to her, and she to us.

God offers us all assistance in so many ways each day. Among the greatest is the gift of Mary, the mother of this sprawling, squabbling Church of imperfect people, the woman who knows our pains and our joys because she lived them too—and who cheerleads for us as we strive to get closer and closer to the One she loves most.

Holy Mary, mother of God, pray for us sinners now and at the hour of our death.

Melanie Rigney

Moved to Save

> On opening it, she looked, and lo, there was a baby boy, crying! She was moved with pity for him and said, "It is one of the Hebrews' children." Exodus 2:6

Though the role of Pharaoh's daughter in the story of Moses gets little press, we can't dismiss that it was a pivotal role in both the rescue and the continued well-being of the infant Moses. At a most unusual sight—a papyrus basket floating down the river—and at a sound that would catch a woman's attention—a helpless, wailing baby—the daughter of Pharaoh is moved with empathy. Perhaps she senses in the scene unfolding before her the bold, creative action of another woman, one who is desperate to save the life of her fragile baby boy.

Pharaoh's daughter notices. She pays attention. She listens to the movement of the Spirit in her heart. She is invested in saving a life, and because of her, the story continues.

Sr. Chris Koellhoffer, I.H.M.

'We're in This Together'

> **There is no one who performs a mighty deed in my name who can at the same time speak ill of me. For whoever is not against us is for us.** Mark 9:39-40

We have a natural tendency to think in terms of us and them. We're right, of course, and they—well, they're wrong, at least to one degree or another. We're better than they are.

But Jesus didn't think in terms of us and them. As long as they were not overtly and obviously against him, as far as Jesus was concerned, they were for him.

Notice, however, that Jesus uses the first person plural: "us." He doesn't say "me." Jesus talks about himself here only in terms of his relationship with his disciples. For Jesus, there was no me and them. He talks about himself in the context of his community of disciples. We might well do the same. To coin a phrase: We're all in this together.

Lord Jesus, help me to think of myself more as a member of your body, the Church.

Mitch Finley

Whom Do I Trust?

The person who is trustworthy in very small matters is also trustworthy in great ones. Luke 16:10

We practice trust all the time. We trust other people—pilots, pharmacists, plumbers, teachers, letter carriers, car mechanics, church ministers, engineers. Closer to home, we trust our spouse, children, friends and neighbors. We trust things too: the chair we sit on, the car we drive, the steps we walk down, the bridge we drive over every day. We would not be able to live a normal life without trust. Trust is the glue that holds the community together. It makes society possible.

That's why dishonesty and betrayal are such serious offenses. They not only damage a personal relationship, they erode the larger community. This gospel reading reminds us of the importance of personal integrity. How trustworthy am I in small and great matters? Whom do I trust? How much do I really trust God?

God, I thank you for all the trustworthy people in my life.

Sr. Melannie Svoboda, S.N.D.

Getting Out of the Way

If then God gave them the same gift he gave to us when we came to believe in the Lord Jesus Christ, who was I to be able to hinder God? Acts 11:17

I do a very good job of hindering God in my life. Not on purpose, of course, but I do. And I'm sure I have lots of company. God knows what is best for us, so why would we obstruct that? Because it's tough to live what we pray: "Thy will be done."

When I am hesitant to welcome a stranger, when I hold back from the urging of my heart to volunteer at my parish, when I fail to be patient, I'm postponing God's work in and through me. We've all felt those taps on the shoulder (sometimes even a shove in the back) from the Holy Spirit, compelling us to act in ways that will form us, and others, into the people we are meant to be.

The more we strive to act like Peter, surrendering our will, the more we will notice and appreciate the gifts that God has given to us all.

Terence Hegarty

GIVE WHAT YOU WANT TO GET

Do to others whatever you would have them do to you.

Matthew 7:12

This is one of Christ's most difficult directives. We somehow seem more inclined to the Old Testament injunction, "An eye for an eye, a tooth for a tooth." You be nasty to me, and I'll be nasty to you!

Suppose that someone misplaces the family car keys. Or a teenage daughter violates her curfew. Or a happy-go-lucky sixth grader forgets to take the red sock out of his jeans pocket before he puts them in the wash. Instead of getting angry, suppose we ask ourselves how we would like to be treated under similar circumstances.

That is what Christ's precept is all about—putting ourselves in the position of the offending other and imagining how we would like to be treated if we were the one committing the offense. It isn't easy, but it's possible with God's help. This is basic Christianity. And those who practice it will likely find personal peace and win the hearts of others to goodness.

Jesus, may I treat others as I hope you will treat me on Judgment Day.

Sr. Mary Terese Donze, A.S.C.

Hearing God's Voice

From behind, a voice shall sound in your ears:
"This is the way; walk in it,"
when you would turn to the right or to the left. Isaiah 30:21

Somehow as I read this incredibly comforting passage, I'm brought back to the crossbar of my big brother's bicycle. He was teaching me about steering, getting the feel of the bike's balance, and becoming confident to find my way and steer straight and true. When I grew big enough to try for myself, I reveled in being able to follow that inner sense and find my path.

The voice that Isaiah speaks of may be a little like that—not coercive or controlling, but teaching and guiding, connecting us with our own inner voice that already is tuned to his. Our eyes cease to be dominant. Instead, we learn anew to hear, to feel and to be guided from within.

The bicycle was a little scary at first, but exciting and compelling. It took me many places I would never have gone without it. Imagine where the voice of the Beloved might take us, as together we learn to listen to its loving power.

Mary Marrocco

GOD IS AMONG US

When Elizabeth heard Mary's greeting, the infant leaped in her womb... Luke 1:41

Christmas celebrates the sacred human moments of birth, of hospitality, of excitement over a future that has unexpectedly and miraculously changed course for Mary, for Elizabeth...for all of us! We often get lost in the daily news, in politics, in self-interest and the convenient worlds of our own making, in financial reports and worries over the safety of loved ones. Advent gently nudges us awake with the message that God has come to us as one of us, living our sorrows and embracing our uncertainties. In this gospel verse, Elizabeth cries out in joy. Following that, we shall hear Mary's song of thanksgiving. On Christmas Eve, we witness the canticle of Zechariah. At midnight Mass, the angels sing their exultant "Gloria!" What will be your hymn of joy for what God has done for us—for you, for me?

Mary, mother of my Lord, visit me as you visited Elizabeth. Quicken in my soul the joy of being in the presence of your Son, the Shepherd who cares for and protects the sheep, the Door to life, the Path to the Father, the Light of the world.

Sr. Kathryn James Hermes, F.S.P.

Our Prayers Are Heard

He who honors his father is gladdened by children,
 and when he prays he is heard.
He who reveres his father will live a long life;
 he obeys the Lord who brings comfort to his mother.

Sirach 3:5-6

When my mother first began to show signs of Alzheimer's disease, I remember one specific phone call. After a few minutes, she suddenly said, "Who is this?" I told her, and she apologized just as quickly. "Oh, I'm just forgetting so much lately." During the same call, she could not remember my birthday. Our family all hoped Mom was just having "senior moments." Instead, it was the beginning of a fundamental shift as children became caregivers for a parent.

Seeing loved ones in failing health can exact an emotional toll. There is sorrow, of course, but anger too—at doctors who can't cure, at loved ones for not healing, at God for not intervening. Overcoming the roiling emotions means going deep within for the patience, compassion, kindness and consideration that will be needed as we assume the duties of caretaker. The grace will be given. Our prayers will be heard.

Paul Pennick

THE VIRTUE OF PATIENCE

The child grew and became strong, filled with wisdom; and the favor of God was upon him. Luke 2:40

This passage reminds me to be patient. After all the exciting events around the conception, birth and presentation of Jesus, he goes home to grow up. The shepherds, the Magi, the choirs of angels all had to just sit back and wait 30 years for Jesus to grow into an adult and take up his mission. In our current culture of cell phones and text messages, many of us can't wait half an hour for anything. And yet, God waited 30 years in a time when those in their late teens were considered adults.

Growth simply takes time, and much of the spiritual journey is waiting on this growth, however much we want to rush into spiritual maturity. It's hard to practice the patience this takes. When I'm frustrated at seeming to have made no progress in compassion or forgiveness after decades of prayer and meditation, I think of God waiting thirty years for Jesus to grow up, and there I find the patience to continue with my prayers.

Aileen O'Donoghue

S-T-R-E-T-C-H!!!

No one pours new wine into old wineskins. Mark 2:22

Those of us accustomed to a cheap bottle of chardonnay may find the image in this gospel reading confusing. New wine will ferment and burst an old, stretched-out wineskin. A new wineskin is needed— one that will stretch with the expanding wine.

In the United States, we remember Dr. Martin Luther King, Jr. There are young people who may have never known or now forgotten that the civil rights movement was a Christian-inspired crusade against racism. It led to the signing of the Civil Rights Act of 1964, but this "new wine" ruptured the "old wineskins" of habits and institutions, leaving many confused, resentful and afraid. People stretched and hurt and cried, "What more must we do?" Yet, thankfully, today the legal separation of "white" and "colored" is unthinkable.

What is today's new wine that stretches us and threatens to burst old wineskins?

Paige Byrne Shortal

Bringing God Forth

**The Mighty One has done great things for me,
and holy is his name.** Luke 1:49

Perhaps, in the end, this is all there is to know. The one who witnesses and proclaims it for us is the one who bears God. Long ago (AD 431), the title of Mother (or Bearer) of God was claimed for Mary by the Church. It's crucial because it tells us that Jesus, who is human, is also God: if Mary is mother of Christ, then she is mother of God. And so God is indelibly wedded to humanity; we can't get him to part from us. We get to eat and drink at his table, for abundant and eternal life.

Saints have charisms, but Mary does not. She has only this, that she carries God and brings him forth into the world. This is everything. This is why all of us, women and men, are called to be like her and are given her as our mother too (see John 19:26).

Mother of God, thank you for carrying God to us and us to God.

Mary Marrocco

Without Delay

Blessed be the God of Shadrach, Meshach, and Abednego, who sent his angel to deliver the servants that trusted in him.

Daniel 3:95

I'm a first-class procrastinator. I'm not proud of this—it's not a positive attribute. But, to one extent or another, nearly everyone is a procrastinator, especially when it comes to facing their own mortality. We tend to live as if we will have many tomorrows.

As Christians, we have no excuse for such behavior. We are told again and again in the gospels how we may die at any moment, how none of us know when the Lord will come again.

Shadrach, Meshach and Abednego had no chance to delay. They each trusted God in the face of what seemed like certain death. But there was no procrastination on God's part—they were immediately delivered unharmed.

Dear Lord, may I, without delay, work to be a worthy servant of yours, today and for all of the tomorrows that you may grant me.

Terence Hegarty

COMMON GROUND

He appointed twelve [whom he also named apostles]...

Mark 3:14

During the Week of Prayer for Christian Unity, observed each January from the feast of St. Peter to the feast of St. Paul, I participate in a local manifestation of Christian unity that we call the Combined Christian Choir, featuring singers from more than 25 congregations. By singing together, we pray to the same God, proclaim our love for the same Lord and profess our common hope in the Spirit's action in our lives. It's fun too.

Years ago, the theme for the week of prayer for unity was taken from 1 Corinthians 15:51-58: "We will all be changed by the victory of our Lord Jesus Christ." Like the apostles in this gospel verse, we are not called because we are already changed. It is the call and our "yes" to the call that transforms us. Let's agree that our "yes" will include finding common ground with all Christians.

Paige Byrne Shortal

'Stocked Up'

If I send them away hungry to their homes, they will collapse on the way... Mark 8:3

When my kids came home from college on the weekend or over a holiday break, I would always take them grocery shopping before they went back to school. I felt better if they were "all stocked up." In between visits, I often sent care packages with homemade cookies, granola bars, nuts and pumpkin or banana bread (family favorites). I knew my kids could buy plenty of food on campus, but, as a mom, I had a need to know they were getting something relatively healthy and something I had made especially for them.

It was more than just food; it was love and care. My kids were journeying away from me, but I wanted them to know there was a place from which they came—a place of love and nourishment. Jesus, the Bread of Life, is that place, and he will never send us away hungry.

Lord, Jesus, please keep me always stocked up with your love and your grace. You are enough for me.

Jennifer Christ

A SOURCE OF HOPE

The LORD is close to the brokenhearted. Psalm 34:19

I was feeling discouraged after a speaker I know told a story that put women in a very negative light. Even though he later apologized, I wondered if he really understood the effect his words had or the deep pain he caused to some of the women attending the seminar on prayer.

While listening to the car radio later that day, I happened to hear an interview with a well-known singer and songwriter. He is a deeply spiritual man, and during the interview, they played a rendition of Psalm 23 he had composed that included feminine imagery to portray the God who cannot be contained in any one image. It was an answer to my prayer and touched me so deeply that my despair and desolation gave way to hope and gratitude for the many ways Christ's spirit continues to dwell on earth and minister to the brokenhearted.

Terri Mifek

EXTRAVAGANT GIFT FOR GOD

Mary...anointed the feet of Jesus and dried them with her hair. John 12:3

Many years ago, I remember passing a florist shop and thinking, "Wouldn't it be great to give some flowers to Our Lady? I'll bet she'd like that." So, I did. I bought the flowers and laid them in front of her statue in our cathedral. When I did, I felt the most wonderful consolation and knew that it made her very happy.

In this reading, Lazarus' sister, Mary, took some very expensive oil and anointed the feet of Jesus. There were those who criticized her, but Jesus did not. He was touched by the love in her heart, symbolized by her aromatic gift, and he welcomed it.

Wouldn't it be wonderful if you were to express your love for God in some way today? You could give an extravagant gift. But the best gift would be your love.

Msgr. Stephen J. Rossetti

SIGNS OF THE KINGDOM

**The community of believers was of one heart and mind, and...
they had everything in common.** Acts 4:32

This passage from the Acts of the Apostles inspired me to join the Church. In my youth, I read the utopian thinkers—those who founded countercultural communities in which people aspired to a different sort of life. I dreamed of a community where instead of competition, cooperation was the norm, and all shared not only their goods, but their ideals, their goals and the work to achieve them. Then I read the gospels and the stories of the early Church, and I knew I'd found home.

Those early Christians ultimately failed at holding everything in common, but the dream lives on in religious communities and lay movements within the Church. This dream is of God, and every attempt to live it is a sign of the kingdom.

Brother Jesus, may there be nothing in my life more important than you and those you place on my path.

Paige Byrne Shortal

Against All Odds, Life Stirs Anew

And Mary said:
"My soul proclaims the greatness of the Lord;
  my spirit rejoices in God my savior." Luke 1:46-47

Today's Scripture rejoices in the most improbable situation. And, even the Old Testament proclamations of salvation are a prelude to Mary's hymn in the doorway with Elizabeth. Where it seemed impossible, new life is stirring.

I need these reassurances. Afraid and deeply disheartened by the world situation, I can lose hope. Surrounded by the specters of escalating violence and endless retaliation, I cannot see a way to peace.

My other dreadings surface: for our planet, for the poor, for all I love who are struggling. I need to hear from these prophets and these two women who are each "impossibly" with child.

Dear God, help my soul to proclaim your greatness. Help my spirit to rejoice during these dark days, trusting in your saving power to bring new life to situations that seem beyond hope.

Patricia Livingston

Our Reliance on Community

> ...there are many parts, yet one body. The eye cannot say to the hand, "I do not need you," nor again the head to the feet, "I do not need you." 1 Corinthians 12:20-21

I recently heard a man boast that he rose to the top of the business world on his own. "I'm a self-made man," he bragged. "I did it all without anybody's help." I wanted to ask him: *Who gave you birth? Who educated you? Who provides the food you eat? Who builds your houses? Who collects your garbage? Who flies and maintains the planes you use? Who buys your products or services? Who monitors your health? Who eases your loneliness?*

The spirit of individualism is sometimes deified in our world today, masking our deep need for others, for community. The truth is, none of us is a self-made person. We all rely on a host of other people to survive, let alone prosper. St. Paul's image of community as a single human body underscores our need to give and receive our gifts with others. Today, let us acknowledge that need and give thanks for all those individuals (known or anonymous) who help make us who we are.

Sr. Melannie Svoboda, S.N.D.

Gamaliel's Wisdom

Gamaliel, a teacher of the law, respected by all the people, stood up... Acts 5:34

Do you ever think about whom you would like to meet in heaven? After meeting my friend Mary (the only person I ever discussed this topic with), I'd like to meet Gamaliel. St. Paul would also be fascinating, but the line in front of him might be pretty long.

Rabbi Gamaliel was a Pharisee and respected teacher of the law. In fact, he was Paul's teacher (Acts 22:3), but Paul didn't always have his teacher's gift for prudence. In this reading from Acts, Gamaliel advises the Sanhedrin to adopt a wait-and-see attitude about the claims of the apostles. He points out that if their claim to be of God is false, then this Christian movement will die of its own accord. But if they are divinely inspired, then the Sanhedrin may find themselves futilely fighting God.

Gamaliel, pray for us, that we may be wise and prudent disciples of Jesus.

Paige Byrne Shortal

Pain Leading Us to Life

> When a woman is in labor, she is in anguish because her hour has arrived; but when she has given birth to a child, she no longer remembers the pain because of her joy that a child has been born into the world. John 16:21

I have never forgotten a scene in a novel where a character who has just gone through a long labor giving birth to her third child reflects on this line of Jesus. She muses, "It is very clear that a man made that statement." The fact is, mothers don't forget the pain. Just go to a baby shower and hear how each story prompts a worse story of something that happened in childbirth until someone finally calls a halt on behalf of the poor pregnant mom whose party it is!

I don't believe we forget the pain. But what we remember becomes a source of strength and hope for other kinds of trials. We remember that pain did not have the final say. The anguish led to life. Joy was born.

Patricia Livingston

God's Rich Harvest

**Thus have you prepared the land...
and your paths overflow with a rich harvest.**

Psalm 65:11, 12

I never noticed nature much before my daughter came along. This is her favorite time of year. She loves rustling through leaves in the garden to find a perfect sun-warmed strawberry. She loves planting sunflowers and hoping they will reach their astonishing height. Maybe we never fully appreciate that our children are other people, wholly separate from us. Her love of living things always catches me off guard because I do not share it. Not really.

I think plants are nice and all. But for her, they are an all-access pass to the God who created them. That's why she still picks dandelions, even though they don't last. That's why she checks for new pea pods every morning, even though she just picked them yesterday. The earth fills her with joy and wonder, just as its creator intended.

Creator God, open my eyes to the wonder of the world you made.

Karla Manternach

In God's Hands

> "Son, why have you done this to us?"... But they did not understand what he said to them. Luke 2:48, 50

How many anxious moments do our children provide us in the course of a lifetime? Plenty. Jesus, like most twelve-year-olds, probably had his share of misunderstandings with Mary and Joseph. This story made it into the gospels. In part, it shows Jesus' exceptional intellectual abilities at such a young age. But also, I think, this passage prepares parents for a time when our children will make decisions, do things and act in ways we won't fully comprehend—or agree with.

We all know that many children abandon the faith, some return later, some never come back. We even blame ourselves: "What did we do wrong?" We worry about what will happen to them. We may not be able to grasp God's plan. There are no easy answers. All we can do is put this heartache in God's loving hands.

Paul Pennick

COMMUNITY OF FAITH

So the other disciples said to [Thomas], "We have seen the Lord." But [Thomas] said to them, "Unless I see the mark of the nails in his hands and put my finger into the nailmarks and put my hand into his side, I will not believe." John 20:25

As I nursed my doubts about faith and fought the urge to skip Mass, I thought about this gospel passage. We are told that Thomas is late showing up. His friends, maybe even some of his family members, greet him with an astonishing story. I know the feeling Thomas must have had at that moment, wondering if these friends were just teasing him because he's late to the party again. Thomas asks for proof of Jesus' return. Physical proof. He probably hears this incredible story a few times from his friends, encouraging Thomas to hang around with them. A week later, in the presence of these friends and family, Thomas experiences the risen Christ.

When I separate myself from the community of believers, my faith falters. The presence of Christ is felt in the Eucharist at Mass and physically in the love of family and friends who strengthen my faith.

Deborah Meister

It's Our Choice

All lives are mine: the life of the parent is like the life of the son, both are mine. Only the one who sins shall die!

Ezekiel 18:4

This reading from Ezekiel questions whether people are punished for the sins of their ancestors or for their own sins. The divine answer is that we begin anew, that we are responsible for our virtue and our sinfulness. Is this good news? Yes and no. If we prefer to wallow in bad habits and blame it on our genetics or upbringing or rotten luck, then it's not such good news. But if we can embrace the freedom we are offered and accept responsibility for our own actions, then it is very good news indeed. We can grow. We can change. This passage concludes: "For I have no pleasure in the death of anyone who dies, [says the] Lord God. Turn back and live!"(verse 32). It's our choice, and it's never too late.

Lord Jesus, show us what we could be and give us a sincere desire for holiness.

Paige Byrne Shortal

Prayer: A Duty, a Joy

He spent the night in prayer to God. …he chose Twelve… power came forth from him… Luke 6:12, 13, 19

My little nieces were engrossed in reading their new books. Just like their grandmother, they adore reading. To my mother, reading is as necessary as eating and breathing. Lately, due to an eye blockage, she has difficulty seeing. She didn't read the newspaper this morning. She couldn't read the recipe she was making. But she picked up a lighted magnifying glass to read morning prayer, explaining, "I've almost memorized it anyway." Watching her, book and glass close to her face, I saw a woman whose strength and grace stem from prayer.

In this way, among others, she's Christ-like. The gospels clearly show how prayerful Jesus was and how he drew on prayer for everything he did. If we desire to be like him, prayer will help take us there. At times, it will feel like a duty; at other times, pure joy. At all times, it's air to breathe and water to drink, ever available, ever sweet.

Mary Marrocco

DIALOGUE WITH THE SPIRIT

He does not ration his gift of the Spirit. John 3:34

I've often thought that the greatest blasphemy against the Holy Spirit is to deny its power. Every now and then, I experience what I like to define as a "God event"—a profound revelation from Scripture, a way of seeing my circumstances in a new light that allows me to carry on with renewed hope. Sometimes a friend will repeat something I told them in a past moment of spiritual enlightenment, and it's as though I'm hearing it for the first time, like God saved the light to be returned to me when I really needed it.

Each event is a little thing that could be explained as a coincidence, but why not give our hearts permission to glory in the mystery of God? Why not suspend doubt and allow that all things are working for God's purpose? Every conversation, interaction and encounter with the Word can be a colloquy with the Spirit of God.

Elizabeth Duffy

GRACE IN THE INTERRUPTIONS

There is need of only one thing. Luke 10:42

In this gospel story, Mary is sitting at the feet of Jesus, listening to his teaching. Martha, who is "burdened with much serving," asks Jesus to tell Mary to help her. Jesus refuses, explaining that he will not deny Mary the "better part" she has chosen. Consider this story in the context of the preceding passage in which we hear about the Good Samaritan who interrupts his journey to care for the stranger on the road. In the case of the needy stranger, immediate action is required. Martha needs to do less activity and, perhaps what she has wanted to do all along, enjoy Jesus' presence. But notice: Both situations call for adjusting plans and responding to the invitation of the moment.

"Pay attention to the interruptions" was the advice from a seasoned pastor to a group of young priests. It's good advice for all of us. Who doesn't find satisfying a day that goes according to plan? But if we learn to find grace in the interruptions, we may find joy in all of our days.

Paige Byrne Shortal

JUST FOR YOU

God gives a home to the forsaken. Psalm 68:7

I often tell my Sunday School students that the Church is here for you. The sanctuary is where God makes himself present in a particular way, just for you.

I always believed that where two or more are gathered in his name, Christ will be present, but I learned out of desperation that Christ is even more generous than that. He binds himself to be present in the Eucharist even for you alone.

At a particularly low point in my life, I feared that I might always be alone. Even if I married, I worried, *would I ever feel truly known and accompanied?* I begged God in eucharistic adoration to make himself present to me: "If you're here, and you are real, show me that I am not alone."

I've kept this prayer in my regular repertoire, not as a prayer of doubt, but because God is generous and he has proven himself in the same way I've asked for daily bread and have been fed. God has supplied comfort and consolation in friendships where I wouldn't have expected to find them, a word in Scripture or spiritual reading when I needed it and his own self in the Eucharist.

Elizabeth Duffy

Nurturing Life

Blessed are those who hear the word of God and observe it.
Luke 11:28

Mary is praised as being both the mother of Jesus and also first among his disciples. At root, these two seemingly different roles are actually one. Her entire being was focused on Jesus. She nurtured him into life and supported him until the very end.

We may ask ourselves what the focus of our lives should be. We want our lives to make a difference. Because Mary's life was centered on Jesus, this humble woman from an obscure town is blessed by all generations. So, too, our lives will make a difference if they are focused on Jesus.

Given our varied vocations, this will take different forms. Parents nurture life in their children. Priests, like me, try to nurture the life of Jesus in others. All of us should nurture life in its many manifestations. If we do so until the end, we, like Mary, shall be blessed.

Msgr. Stephen J. Rossetti

Precious in Your Sight

Rejoice with me because I have found my lost sheep.

Luke 15:6

When he was a preschooler, I let my son play in our fenced-in backyard for short times by himself. Rory loved his sandbox, the garden hose, sticks and rocks. Gifted with an expansive imagination, the backyard was his kingdom! Our large kitchen window faced the yard, so I could easily glance out as I worked, keeping a watchful eye. One day, just that quickly, Rory disappeared! This was impossible! The fence was high, the gate secure. Could someone in less than a minute climb the fence, snatch my child and be gone that quickly? I ran outside, my heart beating wildly. Frantically searching behind every bush and the shed, screaming his name in panic, I could not find my son! I stopped and tried to calm myself. The sound of a little hum caught my attention and led me to the window well, where Rory sat, contentedly tossing stones in the air, listening to them go plunk, plunk.

Lord, help me to remember how much you love us, how precious we are in your sight!

Jennifer Christ

If I'm Too Busy to Pray, I'm Too Busy

The whole town was gathered at the door. Mark 1:33

Jesus is very busy in this passage. After preaching and curing in the synagogue, he comes to Peter's house and cures Peter's mother-in-law. Then he turns his attention to the crowd of townsfolk outside the door, all scrambling for his healing touch. The next morning, Peter and friends interrupt Jesus' prayer to inform him, "Everyone is looking for you."

Many of us can identify with the busy Jesus. At times, we, too, may feel as if hoards of people—family, friends, neighbors, clients, coworkers, parish groups, charitable organizations—are pressing against our door, all seeking our time and attention. At such times, it is good to recall what Jesus did amid the busyness of his daily life: "he...went off to a deserted place, where he prayed" (verse 35). I don't know how busy you are right now, but I do know that you have made time to read this. To me, that's a good sign that prayer is important to you, as it was for Jesus.

Jesus, amid the busyness of my daily life, help me to make time to be with you in prayer.

Sr. Melannie Svoboda, S.N.D.

Learning Mary's Cana Prayer

When the wine ran short, the mother of Jesus said to him, "They have no wine." John 2:3

Mary's emphatic statement at the wedding feast of Cana—"They have no wine"—was a prayer. That prayer was answered in a way that was likely far beyond her expectations—some 150 gallons of choice wine! Mary simply brought her concern to Jesus, without specifying how or when he should respond.

When we make a prayer of petition, we often mention how we would like our prayer answered, but sometimes I like to imitate Mary's Cana-style of praying. Instead of telling the Lord how and when I would like my request answered, I just express what's on my mind and trust that Jesus has a better answer than I do. If a little child has an earache, the child does not designate the cure, but just cries out, "Mama." Mother will know what's best to do. If we have that same deep trust in God, we can express our hurts, fears or any of our concerns and feel assured our loving God will know what is best to do.

Lord Jesus, my good friend is ill. I just wanted to tell you.

Fr. James McKarns

God Is Only a Short Stoop Away

**I have waited, waited for the Lord,
and he stooped toward me and heard my cry.** Psalm 40:2

Sometimes it seems like God isn't paying much attention to me. I have those days and those times in my life (don't you?) when it feels like God is nowhere to be found. I struggle, and I wait for God to help. I suffer, and I wait for God to take away my pain. I doubt, and I wait for God to make things clear to me.

When I find myself thinking that God should reach into my life and change it, I realize that what I really believe is that God is far away from me—that God doesn't much care about me. But Scripture reminds me that God goes out of his way for me, not occasionally, but all the time. God stoops to hear my cries. Even when I'm waiting for God to take action on my behalf, God is already with me. Perhaps God is the one waiting—waiting for me to rise to the occasion, to accept my life as it is or to take my own actions to change it.

God, help me to remember that you are with me always.

Karla Manternach

Responsible for Life

...from a human being, each one, for the blood of another, I will demand an accounting for human life. Genesis 9:5

I've never murdered anyone; I have no children who depend on me; I'm not responsible for any human life, am I? This Scripture suggests that I am responsible—for the lives of all my fellow men and women.

God relies on me for the care of his children. He needs me to be his hands and feet and shoulders for others: widows, orphans—children who precisely aren't my own. Why? Because we are all connected by our common humanity. Like the victim of robbers who was saved by the Good Samaritan, my very life depends on others, even those with whom I may have little in common. As a member of the body of Christ, I am called to work for the needs of every member.

Praise God for the Good Samaritans who work on behalf of life every day.

Lord Jesus, thank you for the gift of life. May my efforts build up those around me, especially those who need it most.

Julia Schloss

RADIATING JOY

**Look to [the Lord] that you may be radiant with joy,
and your faces may not blush with shame.** Psalm 34:6

Happiness is often mistaken for joy. A new dress, a glimpse at the Grand Canyon, a night at the movies may bring fleeting happiness, but not necessarily genuine joy. Joy comes from the depths of a person, lights up their eyes and bubbles out through their whole being. If we would "look to the Lord," we would exude joy, for what else can God radiate?

Whenever I think of joy, I think of Teresa, whose eyes sparkled and whose whole face lit up whenever she spoke of God in her daily life. Whereas the sorrows she experienced in her life may have momentarily dimmed her happiness, they only deepened her joy as well as her trust in all that God was doing in and through her. By temperament, some persons are more effusive than others, but joy transcends temperament. Jesus was God's joy incarnated. When you stop to think about it, is our mission any less lofty?

Grant me the grace this day, Lord, to not only radiate your joy, but to be that joy for those I encounter this day.

Sr. Charleen Hug, S.N.D.

ALWAYS NEAR

...so that people might seek God, even perhaps grope for him and find him, though indeed he is not far from any one of us.

Acts 17:27

Imagine that you're walking in a pitch-dark room. You are slightly hunched over, shuffling your feet and tentatively waving your arms in front of you. And then, you slam your shin on a piece of furniture that was right in front of the light switch!

Feeling like we are lost in this confusing, stressful and often violent world is not at all uncommon. But as people of faith, we are not searching in the dark. We know that God is always close to everyone. Of course, committed, practicing Catholics and Christians still suffer, still lose sight of the truths of the faith.

May we remember today that we don't need to, as some may say, "find ourselves," because we have already found God. May we recall, as St. Paul reassures us here, that God is with us—even on our darkest days. And may we also help those who are "groping" for God to find him.

Terence Hegarty

IS MY FAITHFULNESS FADING?

Faithfulness has disappeared; the word itself is banished from their speech. Jeremiah 7:28

I have two young adult sons who were absorbed years ago with the kinds of decisions that young people have to make—what to major in, what career to follow, what to do in relationships, how to spend their money, etc. They're good young men, but over the years, something dawned on me—as they discussed their problems with me, God hardly ever entered the picture.

As they worked through their decisions, their criteria didn't seem to be much different from any other kid raised without reference to God. Of course, that depressed me, since I had something to do with how they thought about these things. So, in our conversations, I began to try to remedy this, to reintroduce questions of vocation, God's will and purpose into their speech.

And in the process, of course, I had to consider my own goals and hopes for life. It's one thing to worry about my sons' framework, but what about my own?

Lord, you are at the center of my life. Guide me in all I do.

Amy Welborn

Honest and Courageous Prayer

**Many are the troubles of the just man,
but out of them all the Lord delivers him.** Psalm 34:20

The question is not whether we will experience pain, loss and disappointment in our lives, but whether we trust that good can come out of our suffering. So often we are tempted to either deny the pain of our situation or let ourselves become overwhelmed by our problems, lose heart and fall into despair. An elderly woman I knew was dying of cancer. While she had attended church regularly throughout her life and prayed daily, her relationship with God remained reverent but emotionally detached from whatever was happening in her life. When she became terminally ill, she began to honestly express her anger and fear to God for the first time.

To her surprise, she felt heard by God. And, although she was not healed physically, she began to undergo a radical transformation. As she approached the end of her life, she saw not just her faults, but the immensity of God's love. After her death, many of the hospice workers said how deeply touched they were by her honesty, courage and faith.

Lord, may we grow in trust and hope.

Terri Mifek

June 21

Hope in the Darkness

**Wait for the LORD with courage;
be stouthearted, and wait for the LORD.** Psalm 27:14

She was crying when I noticed her, huddled in a corner on the patio of the apartment next to mine. "Do you want to come over?" I asked. I didn't know what happened for her boyfriend to lock her out. The time before, she came home from work a half-hour late. The time before that she lost one of his CDs. He hit her then, smashing the stereo on her hand. Now she grabbed her purse, and I drove her to the domestic violence shelter downtown.

I once asked the director of the shelter if she got discouraged when she sees the same people return again and again. She shook her head slowly. "No. On average, women leave and return to an abusive relationship five times before leaving for good. Each time, I know they are getting closer to being able to do that. It doesn't discourage me; it offers me hope."

Claire J. King

Heavenly and Earthly

If I tell you about earthly things and you do not believe, how will you believe if I tell you about heavenly things? John 3:12

When Nicodemus asks Jesus about heaven, the reply is a rhetorical question with a cryptic message. Jesus does not give the simple answer we tell children who ask, "What is heaven?" Like, "Heaven is paradise, the perfect place in God's presence." Jesus sidesteps the obvious and opens up a whole new lesson plan.

How we, as Christians, understand eternal life seems essential to the way we live our lives and reconcile with death. Jesus calls his followers to live out the gospel on earth as full participants in eternal life. We remain in the dark with Nicodemus when we fail to understand all that Jesus has told us about earthly things—friendship, forgiveness and community—and miss innumerable opportunities to heal, liberate and love.

Deborah Meister

Speaking of the Spirit

...do not worry about how you are to speak or what you are to say... For it will not be you who speak but the Spirit of your Father speaking through you. Matthew 10:19, 20

This is a such an empowering bit of Scripture for me! I have often worried about what to say in certain situations. Many times I have shied away from arguments, convinced that others were more verbally articulate, that they would make me look foolish if I dared contradict them. That translated to my Catholic faith also. How many of us have felt uncomfortable defending our faith or even discussing it with others?

Today's charge to "not worry" gives us a glimpse of the power of the Holy Spirit. We are reminded that the words we use are not ours alone. Knowing that we are God's messengers is especially important as we venture into a world that concurrently shuns religion and is desperate for what the "Spirit of [our] Father" has to say. Are we confident enough to allow the Spirit to say it through us?

Holy Spirit, help me proudly proclaim your message.

Terence Hegarty

When a Hidden God Tips His Hand

Have I been with you for so long a time and you still do not know me, Philip? John 14:9

God sometimes seems to hide—or is hidden—from us. In times of doubt, I find myself asking for a sign of God's existence. Why can't I have a burning bush or get knocked off my feet on the road to Damascus? When I quiet my whining long enough to seek God in prayer, I sense that God, far from hiding, is shouting at us. The problem is that God's shouting is so knitted into ordinariness that we are trying to hear the ocean against the din of the surf.

But now and then, we do hear God's shouting, and for a moment, the world is very different. I recall it happening to me at a stoplight as I watched a handicapped adult awkwardly crossing the street. Tears formed in my eyes as this person's dignity, her shouldering of the reality of herself and getting on with life, robed her with incredible beauty. She did not look at me, but if she had, I suspect that Jesus just might have winked at me with her eye.

Aileen A. O'Donoghue

To Jerusalem's Closed Door We Go

> Because there arose no little dissension and debate by Paul and Barnabas with them, it was decided that Paul, Barnabas, and some of the others should go up to Jerusalem…about this question. Acts 15:2

When my daughter and I have disagreed, I approach her closed door and sometimes just wish that I could let it stay closed, that I wouldn't have to knock, encounter whatever mood she has ready for me and slowly but surely work through it all to the other side. Frankly, I'd rather not do it sometimes. I'd rather just go back downstairs and lose myself in a book. But I can't. The temptation is strong to pretend disagreement doesn't exist, to try to push it in the background, to simply avoid the tough work of reconciliation and understanding.

These early Christians faced an incredibly deep disagreement: the relationship of gentile Christians to Jewish Law. People on both sides had very strong feelings and knew that the way to a solution would require sacrifice. But shared faith in Christ is real faith, and it can't pretend. So up to Jerusalem—or up to that closed door—we go.

Amy Welborn

Forgiveness Is Profoundly Liberating

Her many sins have been forgiven; hence, she has shown great love. Luke 7:47

A long time ago, I hurt somebody. I don't know him anymore, but I suspect that he has never forgiven me. No matter how far the incident recedes into my past, it weighs me down. I feel ever so slightly held hostage by a person I never expect to see again.

I think of this when I read the story of Jesus pardoning the sinful woman. She went a little overboard, I think, with the tears and the hair and the expensive perfume. Now that's lavish gratitude! Wouldn't "thank you" have been enough? Maybe not. I imagine what it would feel like to know that my former friend had forgiven me—that he truly bore me no ill will. No, I wouldn't cry on his feet. But I would feel released. And I would definitely feel grateful.

A long time ago, somebody hurt me. She doesn't know it, but I have never forgiven her. Maybe it's time for me to let it go.

God, help me to forgive.

Karla Manternach

187

TRUST IS COST-EFFECTIVE; WORRY ISN'T

Therefore I tell you, do not worry about your life… Can any of you by worrying add a single moment to your life-span?

Matthew 6:25, 27

Today a cornucopia of pharmaceuticals are designed to eliminate fear, worry, anxiety and sadness from our lives. And while no one would deny the reality of mental illness or its biochemical component, we are sometimes too quick to reach for the pill, the easy fix. Where is it written that we should never feel sad or anxious? Jesus reminds us that worrying accomplishes nothing. There is a saying that "worry is like a rocking chair: it gives you something to do, but it doesn't take you anywhere."

Jesus reminds us of the magnificence of the birds of the air, the wildflowers, the grasses of the field, none of which worry about their existence. They are God's creations as we are God's creations. They are in God's hands as we are in God's hands.

I am your creation, Lord. I am in your hands. Help me to turn my worries over to you.

Heather Wilson

Evaluating Test Results

God put Abraham to the test... Genesis 22:1

I always feel anxious before a test, no matter what kind or how prepared I am. I observe this in others, too: students, job applicants, even hospital patients. There's something about being tested that hits us at our very core. Perhaps the fear stems from our feelings of inadequacy and vulnerability. We remember our past failures and are tempted to despair. But to do so is to fall into a self-fulfilling prophecy. After all, how can we overcome our challenges if we don't pick ourselves up and try again?

This is probably why God "puts us to the test"—without a challenge placed in front of us, we will never know what we are capable of. It's less a matter of proving ourselves to God than an opportunity to gauge (and practice) how we actively demonstrate our faith. With each new test, we have a chance to raise the bar. We're still afraid—and may always be—but with God's grace, the results will continue to improve.

God, give me the courage to take your test when it is before me.

Julia Schloss

'FASTING' AFTER A FRIEND'S WEDDING

Can the wedding guests mourn as long as the bridegroom is with them? The days will come when the bridegroom is taken away from them, and then they will fast. Matthew 9:15

Recently I witnessed the wedding of my closest college friend. Many of my friends have married, but this one hit closer to home. I have known the couple for years; I was there when their friendship turned to courtship. As the maid of honor, I was involved in much of the planning. I went to dress shops; I toured the reception site; I coordinated the attendance of out-of-state guests. I know it wasn't my own wedding, but I felt very much a part of it.

Now that the celebration is over, I feel as if I'm socially fasting. My friend has entered her new life. The time we spend together will be less and different. This fasting can be difficult and lonely, but I must let go, even of what was good, to make room for the new. This is how we prepare for the Great Wedding Feast, where all are united in love to the one true Bridegroom.

Love Incarnate, unite us all and keep us in contact with the ones we love.

Julia Schloss

'Praying With My Pen'

...forget not all [the Lord's] benefits. Psalm 103:2

I am better off than probably 90 percent of the world, but still, I sometimes wake up grumpy for no particular reason. Can't be the job; I'm my own boss and have great clients. My health is reasonably stable, my husband is the best thing that ever happened to me, and the blessing of my sons is co-equal with that of their father. Hearth has some problems, but I am confident that one day we will be able to replace our graduate-student furniture. I suppose occasional nonspecific grumpiness is just part of the human condition.

Sometimes there's no way out of it but through deep breathing and a good night's sleep, but when I can, I get out of the house to the lake or a coffee shop (or a coffee shop on the lake) and bring along a journal. Free of the telephone, email and the ever-present laundry, praying with my pen, by making a list of all the "Lord's benefits" that have been bestowed lately, does wonders to reground me in reality.

Anne Bingham

The Spirit Draws Us to Jesus

The crowds went looking for him, and...tried to prevent him from leaving them. Luke 4:42

Many people were attracted to Jesus, particularly to his healing love for the suffering. Large crowds often hemmed him in, pressing to get close to this special person. In this gospel reading, after Jesus heals, he goes to a deserted place. Even there, people seek him out.

Mother Teresa faithfully mirrored Jesus' love for the sick and the poor. One of the charisms of the order she founded, the Missionaries of Charity, is to seek Jesus in the "distressing disguise of the poor." She did not glamorize poverty or illness, but she stood in the midst of those afflicted and brought the healing presence of Christ. She, too, found herself the center of much attention, and multitudes sought her out.

We also find ourselves drawn to Jesus, to his compassionate love and to those who mirror such divine qualities, like the Mother Teresas of our world. Perhaps it is the Holy Spirit in us, drawing us to all that is good and of God. Let us listen to this Spirit within as it teaches us the ways of God and brings us to the feet of Jesus.

Msgr. Stephen J. Rossetti

A MOTHER'S PAIN AND SORROW

...and you yourself a sword will pierce... Luke 2:35

Our grown children suffer from depression, bullying, eating disorders, divorce, loneliness, financial disaster... The list could go on and on, but for a mother's heart, it is more than a list. It is the prospect of her child's life swirling out of control, of the family's attention and resources being swallowed up by the incalculable and unforgivable. In the temple where she presented her Son to the Lord, Mary's heart was shaken by the vision of what form that "sword" could take. She walked with her child through the joys and pains of his life and stood before the failure and utter disappointment of the crucifixion. Mary somehow had the faith to believe in her Son even as she held his dead body and laid it in a grave. She, above all women, knows a mother's sorrows. If you are sorrowing or you know a mother who is, pick up a life of Mary, your rosary or the Scriptures, and allow her to hold you in your sorrow, as only a mother can.

Sr. Kathryn James Hermes, F.S.P.

Worthy or Not, I Am God's Child

Lord, do not trouble yourself, for I am not worthy to have you enter under my roof. Luke 7:6

I have been that centurion, begging Jesus to heal someone dear to me or that servant who has been healed. But I have come to realize that being "worthy of God" is a misguided concern. Worthy of God? Who could ever be so? It is no longer about that, but about the grace of being adopted as God's own daughters and sons. To bring up my "worthiness" after I know that I am God's very own child is at best irrelevant and at worst a form of hesitancy and ingratitude. As if to second-guess God: "Are you sure you didn't make a mistake here? Did you forget how unworthy I am?"

It is no longer a matter of encountering Jesus' physical body and inviting him to come in; it is more about being that Jesus for others. It is no longer a matter of being told my servant is healed; it is experiencing that healing in myself and in those around me. I still pray those words at Mass, but they have a much deeper meaning than when I first learned to pray them.

Lord, let me experience the same nearness to you as you had with the Father.

Sr. Charleen Hug, S.N.D.

Mission Impossible?

> ...if one has a grievance against another; as the Lord has forgiven you, so must you also do. Colossians 3:13

My son and I attended a recital of organ students. He—who'd just begun lessons—was supposed to be inspired, but instead, teetered on the edge of despair. "I'll never be able to do that," he moaned. I reminded him of all the other things that had once seemed impossible but that he'd now mastered. I could make a list for myself of my own lifelong accomplishments that once seemed insurmountable: reading books without pictures, algebra (how can you do math with letters?), birthing and raising children, writing a whole book, getting through the day of my husband's funeral. And forgiveness. Always forgiveness. Considered from both ends—extending and receiving forgiveness—it can seem an impossible place to reach. *Will they ever forgive me? Can I ever forgive them?* But trusting and imitating the Teacher and reflecting on the stories of mercy reflected in the lives of those who've practiced what he taught, I can see that, no, it's not impossible at all.

Amy Welborn

'The Goodness of Just Being Together'

> At my first defense no one appeared on my behalf, but everyone deserted me. May it not be held against them! But the Lord stood by me and gave me strength... 2 Timothy 4:16-17

When she was young, the child was left in the restroom in a police station. Some trouble had happened that later she could not put into words. Soon, she was adopted and brought to a new country. Still, fear followed her. For years, she would not use the bathroom without hearing familiar voices the whole time.

From our first breath, we reach out for the other. That last night in the garden, Jesus prayed near sleeping companions. The disciples set out on their mission in pairs. Even with Jesus in the tomb, the women could hardly wait to return. Paul is anxious that Timothy hurry back. There is goodness in just being together. No wonder we fear being left behind.

Paul was alone before his accusers. But he was not abandoned. God was present in the courtroom. Facing our worst fears, we come to realize how near you are, God. Show us your presence in times of abandonment.

Jeanne Schuler

'Help Me Proclaim Your Goodness'

> A woman was there who for eighteen years had been crippled by a spirit; she was bent over, completely incapable of standing erect. When Jesus saw her, he called to her and said, "Woman, you are set free of your infirmity." Luke 13:11-12

At times when I have felt "completely incapable of standing erect," I heard Jesus calling me: when I lost my father and two brothers, when I went through a series of surgeries, when I changed my residence, when my prayer itself changed, when I seemed lost in my personal life.

At such times, it is difficult to find words to pray, but that never matters with Jesus. I can't say that I have always responded like this woman who went immediately when Jesus beckoned, but who can resist Jesus' gentle summons for long? And then came the words, "You are set free of your infirmity," of your sorrow, of your pain, of your not feeling at home, of your sense of loss. And then came a freedom I hadn't known before, and I am grateful.

Jesus, I ask for the grace to listen for your voice calling me to you today. Help me to stand erect in your Presence and proclaim your goodness to all I meet.

Sr. Charleen Hug, S.N.D.

All Poverty Brings Divine Mercy

For the Lord hears the poor... Psalm 69:34

On the opposite side of the bathroom door, I heard the muffled sound of my sister's voice. It sounded as though she said something, paused and then repeated herself. Curious, I stepped closer to the door. Her halting speech hung in the air:

"O my God, I am heartily sorry."

The cancer that had metastasized from her breast to her brain left her unable to continue. Again she groped for the next elusive phrase of the prayer we had memorized as children. Her struggle resulted in the repetition of the only phrase memory retained:

"O my God, I am heartily sorry."

Poverty takes many forms, and the psalmist refers not only to those who are materially poor. Circumstances have reduced some of us to a poverty of spirit. Perhaps grief has robbed us of the words to approach God. Others, despite desperate yearning, may remain bereft of any sense of God's nearness. At such times, let us find solace in the assurance that all poverty brings divine mercy.

Phillis Harris-Brooks

UNDER THE SHELTER OF GOD'S WINGS

Hide me in the shadow of your wings... Psalm 17:8

Growing up on a farm, I often saw a mother duck sheltering her ducklings beneath her wings. The sight amused me, for it sometimes looked as if the mother duck had 20 legs! But the sight also moved me, for even as a child, I instinctively knew that the mother duck was protecting her young ones with her own life.

Jesus once compared himself to a mother hen. It's an image we seldom see depicted in religious art, whereas other images—like the Good Shepherd—we see all the time. But the mother hen image has much to offer for our understanding of God's love for us because it connotes oneness, safety, intimacy, tenderness and warmth. If we really believed God loves us in this way, I think we would live our lives less cautiously and with greater freedom and joy.

Jesus, help me to live my faith with greater freedom and joy, knowing I abide in the shelter of your wings.

Sr. Melannie Svoboda, S.N.D.

'Through Prayer'

"Why could we not drive the spirit out?" [Jesus] said to them, "This kind can only come out through prayer." Mark 9:28-29

I tend to think of Jesus as behaving based on his divine nature only. I have to remind myself that Jesus, being both fully human and fully divine, had very human responses. He expressed sorrow and anger, changed his mind and, it appears, was even surprised at times.

This gospel story begins just after the Transfiguration, a beautiful event that clearly revealed Jesus' divine nature to Peter, James and John. And then, immediately afterward, Jesus is faced with such human concerns as bickering and an urgent request from a father on behalf of his ailing son. He seems annoyed that his disciples were unable to drive out the demon. But the message is not that we are expected to accomplish things on our own. On the contrary, Jesus is asking that we, in our human nature, reach out to the divine, just as he did in his lifetime here on earth, "through prayer."

Terence Hegarty

All Things Are Gifts From God

**Bless the Lord, all you works of the Lord,
praise and exalt him above all forever.** Daniel 3:57

Like ferns and fiddler crabs, rainbows and rubber trees, I too am a work of the Lord. But do I bring beauty or laughter or hope or usefulness into the world as they do? Do I truly praise and exalt the Lord, even if just with my being, above all? Or do I just give a small thank you, a little tip of the hat, from time to time—when I can even remember to do that?

Believing that I am among the most blessed of people, I know that my praise and exaltation of God in my life fall far short of "above all," not to mention "forever." Daniel's instruction humbles me beyond measure. But it tells me where I need to go; it sets me on the path to noticing and acknowledging that all things are gifts from God: ferns and fiddler crabs, rainbows and rubber trees. And a loving heart and a fine mind and a true friend and family and people who need us and good work to do.

Where, Lord, would we be without any of these? I will praise you above all, now and forever!

Heather Wilson

Pray the Magnificat With Mary

**My soul proclaims the greatness of the Lord;
my spirit rejoices in God my savior.** Luke 1:46-47

The Magnificat, the beautiful canticle of Mary, rings out across many lands each evening at twilight. It is used at the closing of the Vespers Hour. How appropriate that down through the ages, so many voices have united with Mary's prophetic spirit of grateful praise.

Today, invite Mary's nurturing words of joy to echo in your soul. Let everything that is poor in you receive the good news that God is in your midst. The Magnificat was first proclaimed in that biblical moment known to us as the Visitation. When Mary learned that Elizabeth was pregnant with John, she hastened over the hills to visit her. This meeting was also a recognition of the life abiding in these two wombs. Elizabeth was old; Mary, young. It was a bridge between the Old and New Testaments. The reign of God was breaking into the world.

Stand still and be amazed. Pray the Magnificat with Mary today.

Sr. Macrina Wiederkehr, O.S.B.

WHOLEHEARTED PRAYER

In her bitterness she prayed to the LORD, weeping freely, and made this vow... 1 Samuel 1:10-11

At first glance, Hannah's prayer is familiar territory. How often have I poured out my own troubles to the Lord and made resolutions?

But as I think about my own interior life, I know that my prayers can at times be shallow: a quick prayer in the morning, an exasperated, "Lord, have mercy!" and a brief examination of conscience at night if I don't fall asleep first. Maybe I fulfilled my promise, but maybe not.

Hannah's prayer goes much deeper. No matter what our prayer—petition, contrition, praise or thanksgiving—God seeks our whole heart, our integrity and our willingness to yield to his will. This requires time spent in heart-to-heart conversation.

Dear Lord, I will devote quality time to my prayer today. Let it be the loving, fervent, intimate contact that you desire to have with me.

Rebecca Sande

Making Our Own Way

Everyone who acknowledges me before others I will acknowledge before my heavenly Father. Matthew 10:32

Kateri Tekakwitha, the woman whose life of holiness we honor today, was left partially blind and disfigured at the age of four when smallpox devastated her Native American village, taking the lives of her parents and brother. This strong, faith-filled woman was not a one-dimensional saint as some might romanticize her to be. A product of her own tribal heritage and the colonizing European presence, Kateri strove to embody the gospel of Jesus in a life of prayer, charity and asceticism that may seem strange to us today. Yet the Church offers her to us as a guide and companion on our own journey of holiness, as different as ours may be from our neighbor's path to God. Kateri's life is a reminder that each of us, though part of the Body of Christ and the community of believers, must make our own way to him in fidelity to the call we have each received at baptism.

Claire J. King

Love Is Our Greatest Gift

Do you love me? John 21:16

Parents can provide many important things for their children and still miss the one essential. What is it that children want from their parents more than anything else? They want to be loved.

God provides everything for us. We have a beautiful earth full of rich resources that nourish us, clothe us and promote our life. But what is God's greatest gift to us? His love...made incarnate in Jesus.

Jesus asks Peter three times a critical question: "Do you love me?" Each time, Peter responds, "Yes." Then Jesus gives him a pastoral mission: "Feed my sheep." Peter cannot truly be a pastor and a shepherd like Jesus unless he loves like Jesus. He must love Jesus, and therefore, he must love the people whom he will serve.

Love is the foundation of good parenting. Love is the foundation of a true shepherd. Love is God's greatest gift to us. We work hard each day and give much, but do we love the people around us, and do we show it? This is our greatest gift.

Msgr. Stephen J. Rossetti

A WOMAN OF PRAYER

> Amen, amen, I say to you, no slave is greater than his master nor any messenger greater than the one who sent him. If you understand this, blessed are you if you do it. John 13:16-17

If anyone understood this Scripture passage, it was Catherine of Siena, a complex, bold figure among our noble ancestry, the communion of saints. Although she unflinchingly spoke truth to the heads of Church and State alike, she was deeply aware that the messages she bore did not originate with her but were relayed through her. As a profoundly prayerful woman, she embraced the role of messenger and dignified the role of servant as a powerful witness to the Church by her fidelity to the Word of God in the sanctuary of her conscience.

With Catherine, we pray:

"O Eternal God, receive the sacrifice of my life in this Mystical Body of Holy Church. I have nothing to give except what Thou hast given me."

Claire J. King

CASUAL CONVERSATION

We sat and spoke with the women who had gathered there.

Acts 16:13

It all seems so casual, so commonplace, this reading from Acts. The disciples are traveling from city to city, and the record of their journey sounds like something from a postcard: short, newsy details, including that of a woman named Lydia whose whole household was baptized after she heard Paul speak. The tone is striking to me, however, considering the fact that their mission was to establish Christ's Church on earth!

But God's greatest deeds are often cloaked in simplicity: the gift of a baby, born in a stable of all places; the gift of ordinary bread and wine, become body and blood, soul and divinity of God himself. Is it surprising, then, that the kingdom of God should be built person to person, through casual conversation about the wonders of God, his love for me and mine for him?

Rebecca Sande

LOOK TOWARD MARY

As he blessed them he parted from them and was taken up to heaven. Luke 24:51

I have always had a sad sense of abandonment when I think about the Ascension. "Jesus is gone; what do we do now?" I imagine the apostles saying.

But recently, I received an insight to assuage this feeling. As so often happens, it came from one of my children. My five-year-old daughter and I were at Mass together in a tiny chapel. Behind the chapel's marble altar hung a large, beautiful picture of Our Lady of Guadalupe. Sitting on my lap, my daughter noticed my eyes on the priest giving the homily. She turned my head toward Mary. "Look at her," she whispered. "Look at her always!"

Mary remained after Jesus ascended to his Father, and she gave insight, guidance and tender care to those following him. Remember that she still does the same for us.

Dear Jesus, when I feel that you have disappeared from my sight, remind me to look at Mary.

Rebecca Sande

A STAR NAMED MACRINA

...the stars at their posts
   shine and rejoice.
When he calls them, they answer, "Here we are!"
   shining with joy for their Maker. Baruch 3:34-35

Such a star was St. Macrina the Younger (d. 379), known to us through her brother Gregory of Nyssa! He and their brother, Basil the Great, became key architects of Christian theology and ministry. Gregory says they learned it all from Macrina. On a surprise visit to her, he discovered she was dying. They talked for hours. He beheld her radiance, learning from her about the Trinity and participation in divine life. When she died the next day, he learned more about her. She had brought healing to the suffering. She fed the hungry, treated the poor with dignity, welcomed homeless women into community life.

Gregory was moved to write the Life of Macrina, describing their encounter and the wisdom and theology she taught him, so we can learn from this intelligent, brave, kind woman, who put the gospel into life.

St. Macrina, teach us to know and serve the Lord in each other.

Mary Marrocco

JULY 19

RESPONDING TO THE CALL

"Lord, you know everything; you know that I love you." [Jesus] said to him, "Feed my sheep." John 21:17

I once saw a child throwing a fit outside a grocery store because, evidently, his mother wouldn't give him the candy bar he wanted. His mother rightly said, "I love you, but you're not getting that candy bar." He continued to wail all the way to the car. I'm sure that four-year-old loved his mother, but he had not yet learned that true love requires a response. When we love, we must be willing to respond to the needs of the other. A parent needs to be obeyed.

The same holds true of our relationship with God. If we say we love God but are unwilling to respond to what he asks of us, what good is our love? God's desire is that we love him and care for those around us. We don't get to choose just one of those things. It's a package deal, and our required response is a resounding, "Yes, I will do what you ask of me."

Lord, give me the courage and the strength to respond to your call.

Steve Givens

NEEDING ONE ANOTHER

Fear not, O Zion, be not discouraged! Zephaniah 3:16

The image of Mary and Elizabeth embracing seems an especially fitting one for the Church these days. No doubt these two very human women had their separate reasons to be afraid and weary as they faced the realities of pregnancy, but together, they found joy and courage. At the root of this joy was the presence of Jesus, communicated by the Holy Spirit and recognized even by the baby Elizabeth was carrying. But the two expectant mothers needed each other's support to go forward in faith, hope and love.

Fear and discouragement seem to thrive when we are isolated. Togetherness certainly has its own difficulties at times, but alone, we are stuck within the limits of what we can know and see and feel. With the mutual affirmation and shared faith of the Body of Christ, our horizons widen.

Mary and Elizabeth, pray that we members of the Church might always encourage one another in joy and hope.

Mark Neilsen

MARY, NOT CONTRARY

Jesus said to her, "Mary!" John 20:16

Despite anything that author Dan Brown said in the popular novel *The DaVinci Code,* there's nothing in Scripture that says Mary Magdalene had any children, least of all with Jesus, or even that she was married. But her devotion to Jesus was complete and as committed as any covenant. I guess that's not surprising, considering that Jesus had cast out seven demons that had beset her (Luke 8:2). So Jesus knew he could trust her with the first alert of the resurrection. Jesus has certainly chased demons away from me, no doubt from us all. So, shouldn't I be a faithful witness to the mysteries of the faith? And can't I minister to Jesus, too, especially in the poor, maybe especially to women in need, other Magdalenes? You don't have to be a Dan Brown cover girl to make a difference in this world.

Miguel Dulick

WHO ARE WE CALLED TO BE?

**My help is from the LORD,
who made heaven and earth.** Psalm 121:2

Do modern gadgets and electronics make your life easier? I'm convinced they do for me. As a writer, I have never wished for one second to be back in the days in which one edit to a passage meant having to retype at least one page. Or when sending a submission meant typing, snail-mailing and waiting for months for a response. Or when some topics were impossible to write about because I was nowhere in the vicinity of a good research library.

Has all of this help made me a better writer? Probably not. In some ways, this world of constant, instant information might be hurting me as I am willingly drawn into a world of "quick" rather than "contemplative." And how many hours have I wasted trying to fix computer problems?

Gadgets and more can help me in certain ways, but I can't fool myself into thinking that anything—or anyone—but God can really help me be the person I am called deep within to be.

Lord, you are my help. Teach me wisdom.

Amy Welborn

JULY 23

Searching Out the Salt and Light

Your light must shine before others, that they may see your good deeds and glorify your heavenly Father. Matthew 5:16

Most likely when we hear this gospel, we reflect on our own responsibility to be salt and light. I think I found another message: We are also meant to see the light of others and to give praise to the Father. Negative thinking is a bad habit that can quickly become addictive. Our dark thoughts can be largely preconscious: judgments, criticisms, suspicion, anger, irritation. The darkness of our minds creates anxious feelings, and relationships are slowly soured. Jesus invites us to search out the light, to see the good things others do, to admire the way others salt the earth with God's presence. Filling our memories with light leads to praise, wonder, gratitude, better health and peaceful relationships. If your relationships are not leading you to admiration and gratitude, if your heart is not lifted to the praise of the Father often, you may need to retrain yourself to search out the salt and light around you. Even in dire circumstances, the light can still be shining in some unexpected place.

Sr. Kathryn James Hermes, F.S.P.

Questionable Circumstances

Jesus said in reply, "You do not know what you are asking."

Matthew 20:22

A quick glance at this gospel might lead us to think that the mother of James and John was asking Jesus her question out of selfishness and pride. I don't doubt that those motives were in play. But I also think that her question was rooted in love—the love of a mother. She was asking for a lofty place of honor for her sons, not herself.

She, James and John had spent time with Jesus, learned about his message, experienced firsthand his divine love. Who wouldn't want that to continue? Yes, she likely asked her question out of emotion, and maybe without sufficient discernment and reflection. Maybe she failed to be considerate of others. And certainly she lacked a clear understanding of Jesus' teaching and of eternal life. How often do we petition the Lord under similar circumstances?

Jesus, help me to know what I am asking and strengthen my desire to be a more humble servant.

Terence Hegarty

Memories of Faithful Ones

**Their bodies are buried in peace,
but their name lives on and on.** Sirach 44:14

Although Scripture tells us nothing about Joachim and Anne, who, according to tradition, were the parents of Mary, still we celebrate their memory. Parents are often the recipients of too much praise or blame for the way a child turns out, but to a large extent, each one of us is a product of the love and nurturing that our parents gave us. Mary was well-prepared by her family, common sense tells us, to cooperate fully with God and to help Joseph build a loving home for Jesus.

Someone, perhaps many people, helped you and me hear the Word of God and respond to it. Perhaps it was our parents or grandparents. Perhaps it was other relatives or friends. Take a few moments today to think about how their example and their love has helped you draw closer to God. Remember them, and give thanks.

Generous God, thank you for the people who helped me draw closer to you. May they come to enjoy the fullness of life with you in eternity.

Mark Neilsen

Something to Smile About

You are no longer strangers and sojourners, but you are fellow citizens... Ephesians 2:19

My daughter, a Marine, smiles at me from the photo. She is dressed in full combat gear and carries a formidable weapon. Sun and sand give evidence of the searing desert heat. She stands at the entrance to a tent—a makeshift polling place—realizing that the ultimate sacrifice may be required of her this day as she protects strangers exercising their right to vote. Yes, strangers. The culture, religious practices, language and dress of those she protects differ from her own. Yet on this day, she smiles because she has become a sojourner with them—fellow travelers reaching for some measure of freedom and peace in a war-torn land. The inner struggle for justice within each heart comes from the same Father who created all.

Only the love of Christ and his sacrifice can break down humankind's barriers of race, creed and nation, transforming us from strangers and sojourners to citizens of his heavenly kingdom. His love alone can join us together, building us into his sacred temple.

That's something to smile about!

Nadia Weer

July 27

The Faith of Our Ancestors

That night was known beforehand to our ancestors, so that...they might have courage. Wisdom 18:6

My Grandma Svoboda emigrated from Bohemia to the United States in 1905. She was only 15 years old and was accompanied by two girlfriends her age. With about $25 in her pocket, she crossed the Atlantic in the steerage section of a huge ship. She then passed through Ellis Island and boarded the train to Cleveland, where she was met by her older sister. Grandma never saw her parents or native land again. Instead, she forged a new life in her adopted country, struggling to learn English, cleaning houses, marrying and raising six children. Although she experienced many joys in her life, she also knew "the night." Her first baby was stillborn, she lived through the Great Depression, she saw three sons go off to war (one was severely wounded), and she lost her husband at age 53. I draw great encouragement from my grandmother and other believers who have gone before us in the faith. When darkness came, they clung to God.

God of my ancestors, help me to cling to you.

Sr. Melannie Svoboda, S.N.D.

Jesus Listens to Our Complaints

As they continued their journey he entered a village where a woman whose name was Martha welcomed him. Luke 10:38

Welcoming Jesus into her life, Martha is like the best of us: willingly serving the Lord in the ordinariness of her daily life. All she asks is a little cooperation of those nearest and dearest, particularly her sister Mary. Martha's grievance is reasonable; there is work to be done. Surely Jesus will help her get Mary moving! Jesus listens to Martha's complaint—"Tell her to help me"—but he hears the real problem. Martha is anxious and worried, and no amount of help from Mary is going to change that.

I often find myself "burdened with much serving," not so much because of the amount of work I do, but because of the worry and anxiety that go with it. I, too, have a list of people who ought to be of more help, among them Jesus himself. At least Martha had the courage to take her agenda to Jesus instead of just stewing about it. Because he loved her, Jesus could speak directly to her problem and begin the process of healing.

St. Martha, pray for me that I might really listen to the Lord and be set free of useless worry.

Mark Neilsen

Overcoming Sin

Why do you notice the splinter in your brother's eye, but do not perceive the wooden beam in your own? Luke 6:41

I never read this passage without feeling that it was written precisely for me. My core sins, I'm sorry to say, have changed very little throughout my life. I am arrogant. I am critical. I am ungrateful. I am small. Sure, the particulars change a little. Those sins express themselves differently one day to the next. Still, those are my greatest faults in a nutshell. Sometimes they seem to sound around me like variations on a terrible theme. They are the beam in my eye that I somehow overlook to find fault with everyone around me!

Maybe someday God will relieve me of my sins. Maybe someday humility and generosity and gratitude will pour forth from me like water. More likely, I will labor for the rest of my life. I suppose that is what discipleship is—not being perfect, but striving to become better than we are, today and again tomorrow and all the days after that. Jesus Christ overcame sin for us. Maybe our job is to keep overcoming our own particular sins, as many times as it takes.

Lord God, help me to overcome my sins.

Karla Manternach

Something Better in Mind

Say the word and let my servant be healed. Luke 7:7

Up until the moment my mom passed away from cancer at age 57, I believed God might cure her. Trusting in God's plan and providence, I did all in my power to stir up heaven with prayers for complete healing: said rosary upon rosary, sent friends prayer chains asking for prayer, organized a healing Mass at a shrine known for miracles.

So why, then, did Jesus not heal my mom as he did the centurion's servant? Was my faith not strong enough? Maybe. But I don't think that's it. Spiritual healing happened. And faith was deepened, not abandoned.

It's been six years now since her death, and the pain of her loss is there, but so is peace. I still believe—as I said at her funeral—that God must have something better in mind for her and for us, making our way home. Confidence!

Rebecca Sande

Giving and Receiving

Jesus said, "Amen, amen, I say to you, whoever receives the one I send receives me, and whoever receives me receives the one who sent me." John 13:20

As an elderly widow, my mother often found her days to be long and lonely. She warmly welcomed any visitors who would stop at her home for a cup of coffee. Once when visiting her, I noticed she was preparing for company. When I asked who was coming, she responded, "Oh, there are a couple of missionaries from another church who come every Friday afternoon to visit." Being suspicious of their intentions, and yet knowing they could never convince my mother to leave the Catholic faith, I asked her, "Why do you waste your time with them?" She answered, "Well, we always have a good visit, and I think they like to come here."

Were these missionaries sent by Jesus to cheer up a lonely old woman? Or was this aged Catholic woman sent by Jesus to share her faith with them? Or was it both? We never know during our day when we are the ones sent by Jesus to others, or when we are the ones receiving a messenger sent from God. Maybe we are always both at the same time.

Sr. Ruth Marlene Fox, O.S.B.

UNDER GOD'S LOVING EYE

**Blessed day by day be the Lord,
who bears our burdens; God who is our salvation.**

Psalm 68:20

We often feel weighed down by many burdens. Our shoulders are bowed with the duties of our lives—needy children, aging parents, family illnesses, work, financial concerns, our own physical and emotional needs. We struggle with these burdens.

Yet who really carries these burdens? God is the one who holds the world in existence, who gives new life in this world or calls his children home to the next world. It is God who began the work of creation and God who creates anew each moment of our lives.

God, who in becoming human knew the exact weight of human cares, carries all of our burdens. But we must do our part each day. We must do the work, the caring, the laying of the bricks. God sees the overall tapestry of our lives. We weave the threads of each hour into the pattern. We must let go of the burdens and do our daily weaving with joy and serenity, secure under the loving eye of God.

Lord, may we know that you walk always beside us, sharing our cares and carrying our burdens.

Denise Barker

AUGUST 2

Hostess and Leader

> One of them, a woman named Lydia, a dealer in purple cloth, from the city of Thyatira, a worshiper of God, listened, and the Lord opened her heart to pay attention to what Paul was saying. After she and her household had been baptized, she offered us an invitation, "If you consider me a believer in the Lord, come and stay at my home," and she prevailed on us.
>
> Acts 16:14-15

Tyrian purple dye was a beautiful rich color that didn't fade. It was very expensive to make, leading to its association with imperial dress. Making these textiles was a lucrative business. Most likely, Lydia's husband died. But however it happened, she was a powerful female business leader, having wealth and autonomy. The description "worshiper of God" means she followed the Jewish god without being Jewish. Paul found her, with others, worshipping on the Sabbath. This was Philippi, Macedonia, so with her baptism, Lydia is considered the first European convert to Christianity. She provided hospitality and later, when Paul and Silas are released from jail, they return to her house. She helped bankroll the apostles' travels and the Philippian church. Devotion to St. Lydia has grown; she's symbol of hospitality and of female leadership, in business and the early Church.

Phil Fox Rose

Voicing Concerns

> [My word] shall not return to me void,
>> but shall do my will,
>> achieving the end for which I sent it. Isaiah 55:11

As a parent, I have often been discouraged when I felt that my words to my children were apparently uttered in vain. Stepping on LEGO® pieces barefooted was a painful reminder that someone didn't clean up their toys. Dirty clothes resting on the side of a chair while wet running shoes sat in a doorway were vivid reminders that some of the words from me and my wife did not achieve their desired effect.

I suspect that God may feel the same way about us at times. Try as we may, we regularly fail to listen and adhere to God's word. Our goal as parents is to raise children who will be responsible, caring adults capable of living happy, healthy, faith-filled lives. This reading indicates to me that God's will for us is much the same. We are told very clearly that God's word will achieve "the end for which I sent it" in our lives. We just need to let it.

Terence Hegarty

Carrying the Cross

Whoever does not carry his own cross and come after me cannot be my disciple. Luke 14:27

A friend of mine was pregnant with her fourth child and in the process of building a new home when her husband's army reserve unit was called up for duty in Iraq. The anxiety and strain of their separation showed on her face as the months wore on, and I asked how she was holding up. Her reply was one I'll never forget: "I just want to carry this cross well."

Our response to the crosses in life—our trials and sufferings—makes such a difference! Some may choose to dodge a cross, give up on a commitment or escape through disordered coping mechanisms. Some will take a cross and parcel it out to others through blame or complaints. But some will embrace the cross with the knowledge that Christ has already borne every burden and gives us the grace to be strengthened, rather than crushed, under its weight.

Today Lord, for love of you, I want to bear my cross well.

Rebecca Sande

A Holy Way to God

**A highway will be there,
called the holy way.** Isaiah 35:8

Traveling alone is a daily experience for many people. Even in the moving crowds of buses and subways in a great city, many a commuter travels alone, absorbed in private thoughts, private dreams. We go from place to place in a solitary frame of mind.

The image given in Isaiah of the highway is as challenging as it is beautiful. In an image that highlights the nature of salvation, he writes of a highway on which the redeemed will walk. We are called to move through life together as brothers and sisters toward the city of God. There is no other way there, save the one that can only be traveled with and through each other.

Every person you meet this day is heading somewhere, near or far. Many will be traveling alone, but we are all heading toward the same place, moving toward God. His dwelling place is reached by doing what we can to share the journey with others, be it through prayer or kindness to the weary.

Fr. James Stephen Behrens, O.C.S.O.

We Share in the Joy

> When Elizabeth heard Mary's greeting, the infant leaped in her womb, and Elizabeth, filled with the holy Spirit, cried out in a loud voice and said, "Most blessed are you among women, and blessed is the fruit of your womb." Luke 1:41-42

As we consider this reading, we do well to give thanks for the words of Elizabeth, familiar as they are. In the prayer we call the "Hail Mary," Elizabeth's words follow those of an older translation of the words of the angel Gabriel to Mary. This most common of Catholic prayers is scriptural to its core, and we have Luke's Gospel to thank for the words of Elizabeth that we repeat so often, both as a building block of the much-beloved devotional prayer, the rosary, and as a part of the simple prayer said every day countless times the world over. Endless numbers of Catholics share the joy of Elizabeth and perpetuate her love for Mary, the mother of the Lord.

Lord Jesus, thank you for the gift of your mother, Mary, and the gift of Elizabeth.

Mitch Finley

Praising God in Body and Soul

I was only pouring out my troubles to the Lord. Do not think your handmaid a ne'er-do-well. 1 Samuel 1:15-16

To Eli the priest, the silent motion of Hannah's lips looked like drunken blather. How quickly Eli's perception changed once he realized what she was doing! In fact, Eli joined Hannah in prayer and offered her his own blessing: "Go in peace, and may the God of Israel grant you what you have asked of him" (verse 17).

Like Eli, I sometimes jump to conclusions when I see people worshipping in ways with which I am not familiar—liturgical dance or speaking in tongues, for instance. My reaction stems, in part, from suspecting that these rituals might be inappropriate in certain situations, but another part simply from my personal discomfort with activities that seem flashy or weird to me. As I learn more about these practices, I realize that the intentions behind them are good and that we are all worshipping the same God. So I offer a prayer that in this variety of forms, God may be praised to the fullness of humankind's ability.

Lord, welcome us all into your kingdom, let us praise your name together.

Julia Schloss

EDITH STEIN

It is the LORD who marches before you; he will be with you and will never fail you or forsake you. Deuteronomy 31:8

Often the road to canonization is long and arduous. Sainthood is sometimes bestowed on a person hundreds of years after his or her birth. A particular saint's full story might already be lost or incomplete. Pope John Paul II, one of the most prolific makers of saints in Church history, understood this disconnect. Without damaging the process or neglecting saints from earlier eras, he knew it was important to recognize saints in our time.

The remarkable story of Edith Stein, St. Teresa Benedicta of the Cross, whose feast day we celebrate today, is contemporary, World War II vintage. We know people who lived during that war. We have seen the newsreels and documentaries of the carnage. We are familiar with the death camps, torture and crimes against humanity. Although raised in an orthodox Jewish family, Edith Stein died a Carmelite nun at Auschwitz in 1942. She was canonized in 1987. Her story is alive for us today.

Paul Pennick

MY 'ANGEL OF PRAYER'

Is anyone among you suffering? He should pray. Is anyone in good spirits? He should sing praise. James 5:13

We are asked to pray when we are suffering, to sing when we are in good spirits. If our loved ones are sick, we are to call in faith-filled people. Our joy and sorrow, our sickness and health can be living prayers if we allow ourselves to taste our experiences.

Whether suffering or in good spirits, let us turn to the One who companions both our broken and joyful hearts. We ought never underestimate the power of prayer, even when it appears that nothing is happening, that God has gone to the Bahamas for all we know. Then it's time to believe that every prayer has its own guardian angel. Sometimes the angel of prayer cradles us with tenderness and anoints us with the oil of patience and hope. At other times the angel of prayer skips along beside us, lifting our spirits higher, that we may discover an even deeper joy.

O Angel of Prayer, inspire me to pray always. Guide me through all of life that I may experience God's presence in sickness and in health, in times of suffering, in times of happiness. Teach me that there is no such thing as a lost prayer.

Sr. Macrina Wiederkehr, O.S.B.

Serving in Silence

...and Martha served... John 12:2

I have just finished a whirlwind project under a tight deadline. In such situations I almost always end up, to my embarrassment, talking too hastily, exaggerating and pontificating. The project yanks me away from the space within my spirit where I offer quiet hospitality to Jesus. I end up looking everywhere but into the Lord's quiet eyes.

There is silence within Lazarus' home. Lazarus and his two sisters are welcoming the Lord, paying attention to him, serving him. Not a word is said by any of them.

The others in the scene speak harsh and violent words—they are people who have taken their eyes off him and have started looking in other directions to which their hearts' distorted desire directs them.

Jesus, keep my eyes on you. Even in the whirlwind of daily activities help me grab onto you more tightly, serving you and pouring the oil of my love for you throughout your Church.

Sr. Kathryn James Hermes, F.S.P.

Holiness Is for All

What God has joined together... Matthew 19:6

Jesus gives a profound vision of marriage: man and woman have been created by God for union with each other; thus it is God who joins the spouses together. This is a reality Jane de Chantal knew from experience. She was happily married for several years. When a hunting accident ended her husband's life, she felt, in the intensity of her grief, how great was the love that had grown in her heart toward him. For Jane, the journey toward God did not lead around but right through marriage.

After raising her children, Jane embraced religious life and, with a bishop friend—Francis de Sales—founded an order dedicated to the care of the poor. To a degree that was unusual in their day (around 1600), they stood for the principle that lay people are called to holiness just as much as those in religious life. Jane would remind those among us who are married that the way to holiness lies in our cooperating with God who joins husband and wife more and more deeply to each other.

Kevin Perrotta

YOU BET YOUR LIFE

...to everyone who has, more will be given, but from the one who has not, even what he has will be taken away. Luke 19:26

I struggle with this parable of the gold coins. I definitely identify with the servant who wrapped his one coin in a handkerchief. With a master that unscrupulous and cruel, any gamble is too great. Light shone on the parable for me at a religious education conference held in a casino. The owner had donated the use of the convention facilities. The keynote speaker made a brilliant connection: "This is the perfect venue for us: Faith is a wager! We bet our lives on it."

Life is filled with unavoidable risk. We are called to take "the leap of faith," putting our trust in God with all the courage we have. The more we invest in trust that love is with us, the deeper our faith grows. If we hold back, even what we have can grow weaker.

Beloved God, you are nothing like the master in the parable. I bet my life on that.

Patricia Livingston

Living Where I Really Am

For I do not do the good I want, but I do the evil I do not want.
Romans 7:19

My 89-year-old mother was in a nursing home. She fell and fractured her pelvis and was undergoing intensive physical therapy in an effort to regain her strength and mobility. I went to the nursing home virtually every day to help her eat her meals, to pick up her laundry, to encourage her. I have a demanding full-time ministry besides. I noticed that when I was with my mother, I felt guilty that I was not at work. And when I was at work, I felt guilty that I was not with my mother. I couldn't win. I felt caught in the middle.

Sometimes we find it hard to live where we really are. Instead, we allow regrets for the past to blind us to the joys of the present. Or we let worries about tomorrow keep us from enjoying the blessings of today. A grace to pray for: that I may truly live where I really am—for that is where God is.

God of my past, present and future, I ask for the grace to live where I really am today.

Sr. Melannie Svoboda, S.N.D.

An Empowering God

**The hungry he has filled with good things;
the rich he has sent away empty.** Luke 1:53

Both women were in peculiar situations. Neither should be with child, according to the wisdom of this world. But they welcomed these unexpected events as gifts from God. Their greetings were exuberant. Mary, unwed and pregnant, came to assist her older cousin Elizabeth during the final months. From this young woman comes a hymn of praise for a God whose promises are great.

We read the Magnificat on the feast of the Assumption of Mary. The song reminds us that we do not wait for death to enter into God's presence. We belong to God already. God is not distant, but moves through our lives in the most personal of ways. God also speaks to the world in words far from neutral or detached. The broken and forgotten are lifted up. Those secure in their own sufficiency are strangely empty. The power that seems ultimate collapses before God's truth.

Mary and Elizabeth—young and old—trusted you. God, help me to believe that this promise of transformation and justice includes me and our world today.

Jeanne Schuler

LISTENING BEFORE TALKING

So what I say, I say as the Father told me. John 12:50

An elderly religious sister told me recently that she had a new motto: to speak only what Mary would speak. I thought that was a wonderful guide and something I would like to remember for myself.

Jesus apparently had a similar motto: to speak only what his Father would speak. And what would his Father speak? Jesus must have been listening to his Father all the time so that he would say only what the Father wanted him to say.

If we want to speak only what Mary or Jesus or the Father would speak, we, too, need to be listening to the cues they are trying to give us. If our ears are filled with radio, television or computer chatter, there is not much listening space left to hear God's voice. May God help me to listen so that I may say what he would say.

Sr. Ruth Marlene Fox, O.S.B.

UNLIMITED SERVICE

Whoever wishes to be great among you shall be your servant; whoever wishes to be first among you shall be your slave.

Matthew 20:26-27

On the one hand, we want to be of service. On the other hand, we tend to be very sensitive about being taken advantage of. "By golly, I have my limits. It's about time for someone else to pitch in and help here. I've done my share, now it's somebody else's turn to step up and do their part." Of course, if we all think this way, we will never all be involved together, so the few who are involved begin to think, "Hey, I have my limits..."

Hmm. Rereading those words of Jesus at the top of the page, one fails to see anything about putting limits on one's service. So if everyone puts no limits on their service, everyone will be involved all of the time! Now that sounds like what Jesus is talking about.

Lord Jesus, help me to think of myself as a servant always.

Mitch Finley

DOING GOOD FOR THE RIGHT REASONS

Beware of the scribes, who like to go around in long robes and accept greetings in the marketplaces... Mark 12:38

Read this gospel passage and quietly meditate on what Jesus is saying: the good we do ought to flow from our hearts. Let us be on guard, then, lest we find ourselves doing good things for approval and affirmation from others. We who are created in God's image have been given natural hearts of compassion and love. These are gifts that our Creator gave us "In the Beginning," hoping that we might discover them before the end of our lives. How disappointing it would be to do good things for the wrong reason!

The nameless woman in this gospel reading put her widow's mite into the treasury. She was unconcerned about impressing anyone. She simply gave what she could from the heart. Perhaps we can take her as our spiritual guide for this day.

Jesus, teach me to give my all not to be applauded but because your love in me cannot be contained.

Sr. Macrina Wiederkehr, O.S.B.

A ROOM OF ONE'S OWN

When you pray, go to your inner room... Matthew 6:6

If I had a nickel for every at-home writer who owns up to working in the bathroom because it's the only place the family will leave her alone, I could buy both a muffin and a cup of chai. I've never had to retreat to the porcelain myself, but it has been a challenge to find quiet time when anybody else is in the house. Let's just say that despite decades of encouragement, none of them has yet to grasp the concept of looking behind or under things for the object/paper/item of clothing they've lost.

At a neighborhood Bible study a few years ago, a woman from the Methodist tradition shared a delightful story about John Wesley's wife, Susanna. Beset by toddlers at prayer time, she finally sat down on a chair, explained to her brood that she needed to talk with God right now, and threw her apron over her head. Inner rooms are everywhere; you just need the right look with the right kind of eyes.

Anne Bingham

CLOSING A GAP

He stretched out his hand, touched him, and said, "I will do it. Be made clean." Matthew 8:3

At a parish where I used to work, a friendly woman liked to come for coffee-and-doughnut days. Happy to sit in a warm spot saying hello to people, Doreen generally had a radius of about three feet of empty space around her, mainly because of her smell. Most people instinctively kept a good safe distance. (We learned later she was known to police as "the cat lady": neighbors periodically called them to complain about the dozens of cats she kept.)

One day, my friend Louise went over to this woman and chatted with her. After that, Louise would regularly sit with Doreen, who at first seemed astonished to have a person at such close range. But she loved the attention. At our parish Christmas party, Doreen discovered the crown in her slice of cake and was proclaimed Queen of Christmas. When Louise came over and hugged her, others followed her example!

Louise was Christ, touching the shame in Doreen and transforming it forever. Doreen was Christ, touching the shame in us who kept away from her, and transforming us too.

Mary Marrocco

'Little Girl, Get Up!'

I will extol you, O Lord, for you drew me clear... Psalm 30:2

When the girl fell sleep, her grip on life loosened. She felt herself slipping into darkness. But then a man's voice spoke to her. It was not a voice she recognized. But it was telling her, with an authority she could not disobey, "Little girl, get up!" Feeling suddenly empowered—What's happening?—she opened her eyes, got out of bed and began to walk around the room. Hey, this is great! Mom, Dad, look at me!

Later, did the girl grow up? It seems likely. Did she lead a long, useful life? We hope so. Did she reflect on her experience of hearing the gentle but decisive voice, of awakening and feeling life bursting out within her? Did she remember the man who spoke to her? She must have!

Did she thank God each day with a deep knowledge that every moment was a special gift to her from God? How could she not? Did she pray Psalm 30, as a prayer of thanks? God only knows. But it seems almost as though the psalm was written just for her.

Indeed, it was written for each one of us.

Kevin Perrotta

The Maternal Heart of God

Let them give thanks to the LORD for his mercy... Psalm 107:8

Motherhood is a powerful symbol. It brings to mind caring, nurturing, healing and consolation. In times of stress and distress, people often reach out to a maternal figure.

We associate God with the paternal. We call him "Father," as Jesus instructed us to do. This is good and right. But where does this powerful human figure of the consoling mother come from if not God himself? God is father, yes, but God is also like a consoling mother.

Mary reminds us that God is caring, nurturing, healing and consoling. Today we celebrate Mary as Queen of heaven and of earth. It highlights for us these attributes of God that reside in this beautiful woman whom we call mother. In times of stress and distress, when we call upon our mother, Mary, the maternal heart of God will hear us.

Msgr. Stephen J. Rossetti

Leftovers Again?

...God sent his Son, born of a woman... Galatians 4:4

To outsmart Jesus, it may help to be a woman! Desperate to free her daughter from an evil spirit, a pagan woman barges into Jesus' private party. Even the apostles urge Jesus to answer this annoyance, just to be rid of her. Jesus, who has no one but himself to blame for this drastic breach of protocol, since he deliberately wandered into Syrophoenician territory, finally acknowledges the woman, only to insult her: "It is not right take the food of the children and throw it to the dogs!" (Mark 7:27). In an instant, the woman's superpower—motherhood—takes over. She replies, "Lord, even the dogs under the table eat the children's scraps." Astonished, Jesus now praises her and frees her daughter. He even uses her "leftovers" idea when he shames the apostles in the next chapter for missing the point of the multiplication of the loaves. "How many baskets of fragments? Do you still not understand?" (Mark 8:19-21). So for the Christian, even the scraps are holy!

Miguel Dulick

Opening Our Hearts to Joy

Jesus said to her, "Mary!" John 20:16

Forget the silly novels and the wishful thinking. While the gospels don't tell us much about Mary Magdalene, what they tell us is enough. This woman walked away from her old life to follow Jesus. Why? Because, as Luke tells us, Jesus had freed her from "seven demons"—a way of saying that her problems and her possession were total. Jesus freed her from all that, and so, in gratitude, what could she do but follow him?

And follow him she did—to the cross, when most of the other disciples had disappeared, and then, early on that Sunday morning, to the tomb, expecting nothing but sorrow.

But her faithfulness brings her, as it does all of us, deep joy of the most surprising kind. Jesus is not dead, as she had supposed, but fully alive, calling her name.

Lord Jesus, open my heart to joy, as I hear you call my name.

Amy Welborn

August 24

CHEERFUL GIVING

Each must do as already determined, without sadness or compulsion, for God loves a cheerful giver. 2 Corinthians 9:7

A few years ago, I read the Little House series. In her books, Laura Ingalls Wilder described people from not so long ago who approached their obligations without question or complaint. They did what was theirs to do, did it matter-of-factly and sometimes remarked that "what must be done is best done cheerfully." Even hardship was met squarely and evenly.

Today, a phrase among young people captures this straightforward attitude: "Get over it." Meant to stop people from whining when they face an unpleasant task or circumstance, this phrase is somewhat rude on the surface, but it can also be seen as an invitation to gratitude: "Quit complaining, and look at all that you have to be thankful for!"

It is easy to grumble as we perform our chores. It is harder to thank God that we have people who count on us and the ability to do something for them. St. Paul called this cheerful giving. St. Ignatius of Loyola called it giving without counting the cost. Fundamentally, it is an awareness that even our responsibilities are a gift from God.

Karla Manternach

More Powerful Than Grief

And they were overwhelmed with grief. Matthew 17:23

On the day my brother died, I vividly remember watching his wife and daughters in their grief. My own grief, perhaps because of my age and previous experience with death, was nothing like theirs. They could not speak. They could only cry and hold onto one another and to the rest of us. My brother's loved ones were simply overwhelmed with grief.

Death overwhelms us all because we love life and those who have left us so much. Even those of us who hold steadfastly to our faith can sometimes be overwhelmed by the uncertainty of death and the despair that follows, perhaps because we think that God has forgotten or abandoned us. But with time and prayer and faith, even the most overwhelming grief can and will subside. And miraculously, in the place of our grief and despair, God gives us something that is even more powerful: the overwhelming movement of the Holy Spirit into our lives.

In my moments of grief and everyday anxieties, overwhelm me with your Spirit, Lord.

Steve Givens

REJOICING IN THE GIFTS WE HAVE

Behold, from now on will all ages call me blessed. Luke 1:48

Many people have the notion that humility is a type of groveling, of letting the other guy step on you, of becoming a moral doormat. Compliment such people and they back away from the remark or downgrade the praise. Such people end up either wanting nothing to do with this beautiful Christian virtue or developing their own brand of false humility.

Mary, on the other hand, shows what genuine humility is. When Elizabeth gave Mary the highest praise, instead of denying what her cousin said, Mary added to it, "bragging on" her specialness. But—and this makes all the difference—she gave credit to God as the one "who has done great things for me."

Are you gifted with beautiful eyes, lustrous hair, a charming smile? Do you have athletic ability, artistic talent, culinary deftness or any of a thousand other enviable qualities? Be glad. Admit that you are blessed. Humility is nothing if it is not truth. But inwardly give the credit where it belongs—to God.

Thank you, Lord, for all the special blessings you have sent to me.

Sr. Mary Terese Donze, A.S.C.

Sowing Seeds of Encouragement

From the same mouth come blessing and cursing. This need not be so, my brothers. James 3:10

While making my daily rounds at the nursing home, I find that the time spent with the staff is just as important as the time I spend with the residents. I try to encourage the staff in what they do, to thank them and to ask God's blessings on their work. They almost always respond with a smile, and I like to think that my caring for them lightens their day. When we use our mouths for blessing and encouraging, we bring joy to others.

People in your life can benefit from your blessing and encouragement. Your family members need to know that they are loved and appreciated. If a salesperson or a waiter serves you well, you can offer a word of thanks. The benefits of doing this will come to rest upon you too. Whenever you sow seeds of blessing and encouragement, you reap the joy that comes from offering happiness to others. In this way, we imitate God who blesses us with life and helps us to live it well.

Lord, thank you for your blessings on my life. May I not miss the opportunities to offer blessings to others.

Fr. Kenneth E. Grabner, C.S.C.

God Helps Us Face Our Fears

**My strength and my courage is the Lord,
and he has been my savior.** Isaiah 12:2

My husband and I are having a baby soon. We are thrilled at the prospect of welcoming another child into our family. My last birth, however, went nothing like we had hoped. Our daughter was healthy, but the birth itself was scary and somewhat traumatic. I am full of fear about delivering a baby again.

The other day, as I sat waiting for a prenatal exam, I felt so helpless and afraid about the idea of giving birth that I began to pray. As I prayed, I imagined that God was a midwife—that God would be there to help me when my baby is born. I knew just how God would be in this role: calm, supportive, full of confidence in me and fiercely on my side.

Of course, I don't know what this upcoming birth will be like. But praying about it is reminding me to trust in God when I have to face my fears. Remembering that God will be with me gives me strength and a new sense of courage. It is one thing I know I can be sure of that day...and every day after that.

Karla Manternach

Give Credit Where Credit Is Due

Accompanying him were the Twelve and some women who had been cured of evil spirits and infirmities... Luke 8:1-2

In the modern way of seeing, religion is simply one part of life among many. It is the part in which we find meaning and inner peace and perhaps some moral guidance. We find time for it, we schedule it, we give it priority.

Contemplating Luke's simple, straightforward description of Jesus' female disciples, I can't help but be startled by the contrast between their stance and mine. There is no fitting faith into a busy life here; there is simply a life turned over to Jesus completely, and in gratitude. A startling move for the time, since women did not ordinarily leave their homes to follow itinerant rabbis. Radical, bold and total, not grudging or duty-bound. What's the difference? I think it lies in our sense of who we think deserves the credit. Mary Magdalene, Joanna and Susanna were transformed by Jesus, and they knew it. Who do I think deserves the credit for my life and its blessings?

Lord Jesus, in gratitude, I give you more of my heart. Give me the courage to hand it all over to you.

Amy Welborn

The Treasure of Prayer

For where your treasure is, there also will your heart be.

Matthew 6:21

I held the hand of my eighty-two-year-old mother as she lay dying. I remembered how many times she had held my hand to cross, to go shopping, to go to church, especially for novenas. She had great faith in prayer.

I had always thought her greatest treasure was her family, but as she became ill, she seemed to become detached from us. I realized that with her ebbing vitality she did not have the energy to give us her attention. She could focus now only on the God who had always been first with her.

I prayed the rosary as her breaths became more and more shallow and further apart. Then she simply stopped breathing. There was no great struggle, just peace and serenity. I was awed by the mystery of death, sad that she had left us, but happy that her heart had finally returned to her treasure.

Joan Zrilich

The Needy Need Me to Be a Neighbor

Which of these three, in your opinion, was neighbor to the robbers' victim? Luke 10:36

Like the man who asked Jesus, "Who is my neighbor?" I also want to narrowly define "neighbor," squeezing it down into the few people and interruptions I can reasonably deal with. Jesus, however, is not interested in that question and doesn't even answer it.

After his tale of the man beaten and left for dead on the side of the road, Jesus asks a different question: "In this story, who has been the neighbor?" It is not a question of selecting those to whom I will dole out a few moments of compassion during the day. It is a matter of realizing that I need to become the neighbor who, despite inconvenience, drops everything to attend to another's need. In fact, it is precisely on this that my final judgment will be based: feeding the hungry, visiting the imprisoned, clothing the naked.

Lord, I beg you, teach me to be neighborly.

Sr. Kathryn James Hermes, F.S.P.

A LESSON IN DETACHMENT

It is easier for a camel to pass through [the] eye of [a] needle than for one who is rich to enter the kingdom of God.

Mark 10:25

Several months before my mother died, she gave away all her possessions. From her room in the nursing home she said, "I won't have need of them anymore." I marveled at my mother's detachment as she watched her children and grandchildren systematically divide up her belongings. Interestingly, the most sought after items were not the items of greatest monetary worth, but those of greatest sentimental value: Mom's cookbook, prayerbook, rolling pin, cookie jar, etc.

Mom gave away her belongings not grudgingly but warmly. She seemed delighted that her descendents were eager to have those things that would forever remind them of her. My mother had lived a simple life for over 90 years. Hence, she was very prepared to carry out this final divestment of her earthly goods. It was a grace given to her by God who revels in doing impossible things.

Loving God, give me the grace to divest myself of something I am clinging to today.

Sr. Melannie Svoboda, S.N.D.

In Giving, We Receive

Elijah said to her, "Do not be afraid. Go and do as you propose. But first make me a little cake and bring it to me. Then you can prepare something for yourself and your son."

1 Kings 17:13

Picture this: tonight you're reviewing your day. You recall someone's request for help with a problem. You replied: "Nope, I'm too busy." Now, looking back, do you think to yourself, "Yes! I was selfish. What a great day!" Or do you regret your selfishness, acknowledging that, yes, you were busy, but that you could have spared some of your time?

Like the widow who was down to her last bit of food, oil and water, our resources are always limited in some fashion. Still, in sharing what little she had at the prophet's request, she was blessed with miraculous abundance, the story continues, for another entire year even though scarcity and drought continued around her.

However difficult it might be, we know it's true: we reap what we sow; it is in giving that we receive; it is by sharing that we are blessed with abundance.

Now that's how to live if you want to nod off easily tonight.

Fr. James Krings

September 3

The Courage to Be Compassionate

Amen, I say to you, whatever you did for one of these least brothers of mine, you did for me. Matthew 25:40

Perhaps more than anyone else this past century, Mother Teresa showed us what it meant to have "eyes of faith," to see in the face of others the face of Jesus. Nurtured by her daily reception of Communion, she brought the love of Jesus to the least of Jesus' sisters and brothers. And so can we. In fact, we must, Jesus says, if we want to be in communion with him now and in the life to come. Jesus says that we will find and serve him in the lives of the hungry, homeless, sick and imprisoned. But as their numbers seem to grow each year, so, too, our fears of getting involved seem to grow. Our compassion is challenged by news reports of startling images of poverty and violence. We need to learn from Mother Teresa how to find the faith and courage to reach out to those who hurt. She made time each day for prayer and the Eucharist to savor God's presence and love. And she had sisters and brothers to walk with into the risky life of compassionate service.

Jesus, help us make prayer, Communion, a community of disciples and compassion the core of our lives, so that we might be with you now and forever.

James McGinnis

What Is the Prayer of My True Self?

They were eating and drinking, marrying and giving in marriage up to the day... Luke 17:27

As Beatle John Lennon said, "Life is what happens to you while you're busy making other plans." So often the big events happen on ordinary days when nothing much is expected. I've found this to also be true about prayer: extraordinary moments of connection with God most often happen when I'm not praying...God happening while I'm making other plans.

I wonder if I'm somehow praying while I think I'm making other plans. How do I know when I'm in prayer? How does prayer feel? My first thought is that in prayer I should feel holy and somehow different from how I normally feel. When I feel most like myself, I figure I'm not praying, yet that's when I'm likely to have a deeply spiritual experience.

So perhaps the deepest prayer is achieved when we are simply completely and truly ourselves, and that our "ordinary" selves on "ordinary" days are not ordinary at all.

Aileen O'Donoghue

Turning Anxieties into Prayer

Have no anxiety at all, but in everything, by prayer and petition, with thanksgiving, make your requests known to God.

Philippians 4:6

At first, St. Paul's admonition seems unrealistic: "have no anxiety at all"? Who among us can go even one day without worrying about something? Perhaps we are worried about a loved one, our health, our financial security, some worthwhile project we're working on, a terrorist attack, global warming or our own failures and shortcomings. But St. Paul adds this: "by prayer and petition...make your requests known to God." In other words, turn your anxieties into prayer.

Today let us list our major anxieties—perhaps even in writing. Then let us turn each anxiety into a petition to God, ending with something like this:

These are my major anxieties today, God. I entrust them all to you. If there is some specific action you want me to take with regard to any of these anxieties, please let me know. Thank you! Amen.

Sr. Melannie Svoboda, S.N.D.

MARY, THE MODEL DOER OF GOD'S WILL

Blessed are you who believed that what was spoken to you by the Lord would be fulfilled. Luke 1:45

Thus is Mary exalted by her cousin Elizabeth. Think of it: from the moment the angel tells Mary that she, a virgin, will conceive and bear a son to her lonely vigil at the foot of the cross, Mary never wavers in her faith in the Lord. She never hesitates in her part of the fulfillment of God's plan. What an amazing role model she is for us!

When we want to know what's coming next, when we demand explanations and signs, when we bargain, cajole or hesitate on our faith journey, let us remember Mary who never stammered, stumbled or sidestepped when asked to do God's will.

Pray for us, Mary, now and at the hour of our death.

Heather Wilson

IMITATING MARY'S FAITH

We know that all things work for good for those who love God... Romans 8:28

My mother had a great devotion to Mary. She named her first girl Mary Ann. In her living room, she had a three-foot statue of Mary and always kept a small vase of fresh flowers in front of it. Mom prayed the rosary every day too. Her devotion also included talking with Mary in prayer—woman to woman, wife to wife, mother to mother, friend to friend. But most of all, her devotion consisted in imitating Mary's faith, especially when things were difficult. Many times when circumstances were painful or confusing, I heard my mother say (sometimes even with tears), "The good Lord knows what he's doing." Despite the pain and confusion, my mother hung on and trusted—as Mary did—that all things work for good.

Today we commemorate not necessarily an actual date, for no one really knows Mary's true birthday. But we celebrate an actual woman, a real believer.

Mary, mother and disciple of Jesus, help me to imitate your very real faith.

Sr. Melanie Svoboda, S.N.D.

Speak What's in Your Heart

[Anna] never left the temple, but worshiped night and day with fasting and prayer. And coming forward at that very time... Luke 2:37-38

Sometimes our days can seem more about emptiness, failure and letdown than about fulfillment and accomplishment. A pause in our regular schedule pulls back the veil over our inner lives, but instead of fullness and joy, we may become more aware of absence, anger, betrayal and even deadness. The angels proclaim glory, but how can we poor little shepherds, alone on the dark hillside, feel glory in the here-and-now? Anna herself gives us an answer. She comes forward; she gives thanks; she speaks about the child Jesus. Can we, today, come forward to each other? Can we give thanks, even amidst sorrow and pain? Can we take the risk to speak out of love, knowing our love is imperfect, our words flawed, our understanding limited?

Christ is the Word of God among us. But we are his little words, too, and he encourages us to speak what's in our hearts. Someone near you is longing to hear it!

Mary Marrocco

Thank You, God, for Everything!

**I will praise the LORD with all my heart
in the company and assembly of the just.** Psalm 111:1

Today is someone's birthday. Or anniversary. It's a day to start a new job or begin retirement. For some, it is a special day; for others, an ordinary day. But like every day, it offers many opportunities to give thanks to God—for the air we breathe, the food we eat, the sounds we hear, the people we hug; for the love that grows in our hearts and springs forth to touch so many; for the faith that nourishes our souls and the hope that gives meaning to all that we do; for a baby's cry, a child's energy, a teen's enthusiasm, a worker's skill, an older person's wisdom and memories.

Even if we made a list each day for a year of 100 things for which to thank God, we would not begin to cover all that God has given us. God has surrounded and filled us with a never-ending abundance of good things. What joy there is in truly realizing this! What freedom from fret and worry! Let us give thanks—in solitary prayer, at Mass, with family and friends, in song and dance, with laughter or tears. Thank you, God, for everything!

Charlotte A. Rancilio

A Terrifying Awareness

And he has made the world firm, not to be moved. Psalm 93:1

Do you remember the moment, as a child, when you realized your parents weren't impervious to death and weakness? That they could make mistakes, and even be taken away? It's a life-changing moment, itself a death and a birth. A source of chronic anxiety for our era is that the world we live in is vulnerable. Like children coming to new consciousness of their guardians' mortality, we as a society are wrestling to understand that our environment—that which holds us safe—is in danger. We can't be sure, now, that the world will stand in place tomorrow or the day after that.

Could this terrifying awareness be bringing something new? God's creative activity is different from that of, say, a painter, who makes a painting and then moves on. God creates in every moment, breathing life into each of us, into all that is. Otherwise, we would cease to exist. The evidence of his astonishing promise— that the world will surely stand in place—is here, now, waiting for us to see.

Lord, open me to your eternal life, sustaining everything around me.

Mary Marrocco

September 11

Opening House and Heart

> After [Lydia] and her household had been baptized, she offered us an invitation, "If you consider me a believer in the Lord, come and stay at my home," and she prevailed on us.
>
> Acts 16:15

I have a thing about houseguests...being one or having one. I grudgingly think the three-day rule applies. I get anxious before the arrival of a houseguest, thinking in classic "Martha style" about all the things I have to do: clean sheets, grocery store, fresh flowers, bake something, plan a menu, figure out activities, etc. If I already have a lot on my plate at the time, I can feel put out before they ever arrive. But I always end up having fun and regretting my first impulse. Lydia, on the other hand, not only asks, she persuades Timothy, Paul and Silas to stay at her house. There isn't an ounce of resistance in her heart, and these men are virtual strangers to her. The Lord opened her heart to respond to Paul's message, and her welcoming actions exemplified that openness.

Whether it's a matter of opening up my house or my heart, I can see that I am likewise called to respond, as a believer, with openness, hospitality and love.

Kristin Armstrong

The Faith of Children

I assure you that whoever does not accept the kingdom of God like a child shall not enter into it. Mark 10:15

Sometimes I find it very painful to watch a small child at play or in its mother's or father's embrace. There is such complete trust, such delight, such sweetness that I find myself grieving over my own children and their lost innocence. The teenage years, are, one hopes, a prelude to better things. But for many families, they bring with them chaos and discord. I find myself remembering children's pleasure in little things—their spontaneity, their openness to mystery and beauty, their simple faith. I realize that a major task of their adult life will be to recover the very qualities that were seemingly lost in adolescence.

Jesus holds up a small child as a model of what it means to be a disciple. Lacking sophistication, this child sees things as they are and is not afraid to name them. Lacking ulterior motives, this child speaks the truth without trying to impress others or to manipulate them. Lacking the need to be in control, this child is willing to find the reign of God in the present moment, not according to some preconceived plan, but however it presents itself.

Elizabeth-Anne Vanek

September 13

All Different, All Jesus

For I resolved to know nothing while I was with you except Jesus Christ, and him crucified. 1 Corinthians 2:2

Let me tell you about all the crosses in my house. In the living room, there's the simple, yet vivid crucifix from Mexico. In the next room hangs a brightly painted ceramic cross, swirling with primary colors, from Sicily. Look on the shelf, and we're back in Mexico—a small crucifix completely woven from palm branches—a Palm Sunday tradition there. In my room, I look near my desk and I see the plain wooden cross, part of the monk-made casket in which my husband was buried. The cross was on the lid, and fashioned to be removed and kept above ground by those still here. And over there by the door is the risen Christ—odd considering how traditional my mother was—that was my first Communion gift decades ago. All different, all the same. All Jesus, in suffering and love, with me on this journey always.

Amy Welborn

LIKE MOTHER,
LIKE SON

Behold, this child is destined for the fall and rise of many in Israel, and to be a sign that will be contradicted (and you yourself a sword will pierce)... Luke 2:34-35

Our Lady of Sorrows is my patron saint; "Melanie" in Greek means, "one who mourns." For many years, I have enjoyed a special affinity with this feast.

Tradition tells us Mary endured seven major sorrows—from the flight into Egypt to the crucifixion, death and burial of Jesus. As I reflect on her "seven dolors," I notice that Mary's sorrows were a direct result of her relationship with Jesus. Perhaps this feast should serve as a warning to us that we risk sorrows, disruptions and heartaches if we align ourselves closely with Mary's son. Mary's son. When Jesus was dying on the cross, his last words, "Into your hands I commend my spirit," were from Psalm 31. Jesus may well have learned these words from his mother. After all, they echo what she said at the Annunciation: "Be it done unto me according to your word." Such words guided Mary through times of joy as well as adversity. Like mother, like son. Like son, like mother.

Mary, woman of joy and sorrow, help me to be more like you.

Sr. Melannie Svoboda, S.N.D.

SEPTEMBER 15

'Close to Jesus to the Last'

> When Jesus saw his mother and the disciple there whom he loved, he said to his mother, "Woman, behold, your son." Then he said to the disciple, "Behold, your mother."
>
> John 19:26-27

Journalists' photographs depicting tragic scenes the world over seem most eloquent when they portray a mother's grief. No matter what language is spoken to give utterance to the heart's anguish, the camera riveted to the face of a mother mourning her child in the aftermath of great loss is understood by people everywhere. For centuries, the Church has sung the Stabat Mater Dolorosa, a doleful hymn of remembrance for Mary's very real, very human pain. In its haunting melody, one can picture readily both the desperate sadness and unflinching faith of the Mother of Jesus, holding in her arms the lifeless body of her beloved Son. "At the cross her station keeping/stood the mournful mother weeping/close to Jesus to the last."

Claire J. King

God's Messy, Beautiful House

So then you are no longer strangers and sojourners, but you are fellow citizens with the holy ones and members of the household of God... Ephesians 2:19

We travel quite a bit and so have the opportunity to attend churches all around the country. Often, at the beginning of Mass, the celebrant invites visitors to make themselves known by raising their hands or even announcing where they're from. A very well-intentioned practice, to be sure, but one that always makes us think a little.

When we attend another Catholic church, are we really "visitors?" After all, we're not baptized into a particular parish, we're baptized into Christ through his Church. So aren't I actually a parishioner at every parish in the world, from St. Peter's to Mumbai to Sao Paulo? I think I am, and so are you. That's a pretty amazing and humbling thought to me—that when we're at Mass together, there are no visitors or strangers. There's only a chance to welcome another brother or sister into another room in this huge, messy but beautiful household of God.

Lord, open my heart to all my sisters and brothers.

Amy Welborn

September 17

Divine Words Are Like Jewels

Take these words of mine into your heart and soul. Bind them at your wrist as a sign, and let them be a pendant on your forehead. Deuteronomy 11:18

Devotional jewelry, charms and beads hold much power for the person they belong to. The words and memories associated with each item are strong reminders of the spiritual truth it symbolizes. This is seen even in the secular society in its selling of "best friends" charms and the passing down of family heirlooms.

But this passage brings to mind another type of devotional "jewelry": my rosary beads. I was once told that one should never buy one's own rosary; it should be given and received as a gift. And I must say I do feel a deep connection with the giver of each rosary I pray with. Each of mine comes from a different person close to my heart and was bought in a different country. As I recite the words, the string of beads becomes a story, a relationship, a way to express my love for God and neighbor, tangibly and intangibly.

Julia Schloss

God's Way Of Hearing

Shall he who shaped the ear not hear? Psalm 94:9

When I'm teaching, sometimes I wonder if anyone is actually listening to anything I'm saying. So far I've resisted the urge to say something truly outrageous —"Pope declares Fourth Person of the Trinity"—just to see if they'll notice what they're writing.

Since we're so adept at not hearing, it's natural we suspect God of not hearing. After all, evil and injustice are everywhere, and God seems oblivious. We may be tempted to do outrageous things like Cool Hand Luke's standing in the thunderstorm, shouting: "Go ahead and strike me—anything, just so I know you're there."

What does God hear? He not only hears everything, but he is the hearing itself (he shaped the ear). I suspect his answer, or his silence, his way of hearing and his way of speaking, shapes us too. We may not know what we're being shaped into, and the shaping is painful at times or perplexing. But we can help one another, and we have prayer as our ally—two of life's most beautiful realities. God leads us to one another, and to himself.

Mary Marrocco

'Great Is Your Faith!'

> The woman came and did him homage, saying, "Lord, help
> me." He said in reply, "It is not right to take the food of the
> children and throw it to the dogs." She said, "Please, Lord, for
> even the dogs eat the scraps that fall from the table of their
> masters." Then Jesus said to her in reply, "O woman, great is
> your faith! Let it be done for you as you wish."
>
> Matthew 15:25-28

Jesus' encounter with the Syrophoenecian woman echoes a troubling line from the teachings after the Sermon on the Mount: "Do not give what is holy to dogs, or throw your pearls before swine" (Matthew 7:6). How can this be the same Jesus who tells the story of the Good Samaritan (Luke 10:25-37), teaching that you have a responsibility to every person as a fellow child of God? Here he is equating foreigners with dogs. At first glance, I don't like this Jesus at all. There is an explanation though, which some will find just as challenging. That is, that Jesus is learning. In his cultural context, his reaction would be normal. Asked to help a non-Jew, he says, "Why should I care about that?" But the woman, through her genuine faith, perhaps helps him to realize that she is his concern too. And Jesus' heart opens.

Phil Fox Rose

Becoming a Model of Faith

The kingdom of heaven is like a mustard seed…

Matthew 13:31

Seeds have always served as inspiration for me. When we are truly attentive, how can we not stand in awe before a seed? What a mystery it is with its potential to break open and pour out life! How amazing to watch the growth of tiny things!

How can something so small become so magnificent? Imagine for a moment how small you were on the day of your birth. You, too, grew from a seed. Like the mustard seed you are filled with budding possibilities for growth.

Imagine that today is your birthday. Rejoice in the truth that God breathed upon the tiny seed of you. God smiled upon your smallness and you blossomed into a wondrous tree of life. You, too, are a sign of the kingdom of God. The leaven of your little life lived with faithfulness can assist others in rising to the greatness God desires for them. Happy birthday, you beautiful tree of life.

Sr. Macrina Wiederkehr, O.S.B.

IF YOU WANT IT

Jesus said to him, "Rise, take up your mat, and walk."

John 5:8

I am thinking about the lame man, so close to the healing waters, and Jesus asks him, do you want to be well? For 38 years the lame man has been making excuses. "No one will help me. Others get there first."

Wellness in Christ is different from self-help. Self-help methodologies invite us to find the right combination of efforts that will transform our lives. But their effects are rarely long lasting and often, their rewards fail to satisfy.

Belief in Christ is not a solution; it is a communion, an opportunity to bathe heartily and frequently in the waters of Christ's mercy. If you want it, there is enough mercy to sustain a lifetime in faith.

Elizabeth Duffy

The Persistent Heart

Ask and you will receive; seek and you will find; knock and the door will be opened to you. Luke 11:9

More than a decade ago, I experienced the death of a dear friend who was a shining light and mentor to me. Over several years, Chrissie suffered the debilitating effects of a recurrence of cancer. Though her illness progressively limited her mobility and energy, she summoned the strength to remain deeply engaged in the lives of those she loved and to spend her last days, as she had spent every day, immersed in prayer. When she could do little else, she clasped her rosary as she interceded over and over again for the needs of our world, both the small and the local, the large and the global. To her last breath, she called on our loving God with serene confidence.

When Jesus' disciples requested, "Teach us to pray," Jesus urged them to shape their prayer with this same deep trust in a compassionate God. Jesus urges us also to be persistent and unashamed as we keep on asking, keep on seeking, keep on knocking. Let us commit ourselves to be faithful to pray as Jesus invites us: unceasingly, undeterred by seeming silence and unshaken in the hope of God's promise.

Sr. Chris Koellhoffer, I.H.M.

God Wants to Be Wanted

For in Christ Jesus, [what] counts…[is] faith working through love. Galatians 5:6

As a celibate priest and a psychologist, I spend a lot of time with married couples, often as a confidant and a counselor. I admire those who have the courage to enter into a lifelong commitment to marriage. They witness to what is most noble in humanity.

Conflicts and challenges abound in all relationships, but especially in marriage where emotions run deepest. But there is a common problem, perhaps the problem that surfaces most often. It is simple: people desire to be truly loved and wanted by the other. All the time, gifts and affections directed toward the other really amount to one simple statement: "I love you, and I want you in my life." And when a spouse does not feel wanted, troubles begin.

What is it that God desires from us? Nothing different. God wants our love. God desires, not so much our sacrifices and external signs, God wants our hearts. We ought not to be surprised. God made us just like himself.

Lord Jesus, I want you, I need you, I love you.

Msgr. Stephen J. Rossetti

First of All, Be Kind

Be kind to one another, compassionate, forgiving one another as God has forgiven you in Christ. Ephesians 4:32

I had a friend who was a marriage counselor. He would tell me about sessions with couples squabbling over almost every large and small thing. Inevitably some of these marriages would fail. But with some relationships he truly felt he made a difference. "What does work?" I asked. "What do you tell these people?"

Years of training, thousands of hours with hundreds of people, taught him one simple, basic truth about successful human relationships: "First of all," he said, "you need to be kind to one another." He was amazed at how often this tiny bit of advice turned a troubled marriage into a happy partnership.

We know that kindness will not heal all wounds, nor will it solve every disagreement. But don't we also know that kindness is a variant of love? Every act of kindness is a nugget of God's grace given to us freely, something we can pass on to others.

Lord Jesus, help me to be kind, compassionate and forgiving.

Paul Pennick

PERSISTENT GROWTH

Draw your strength from the Lord and from his mighty power.

Ephesians 6:10

Almost any day, I can look down and see small seedlings that have made their way to the light of day. It is not unusual to see the beginnings of trees emerging through concrete. Their persistent growth astonishes me. Concrete cracks and gives way to a little green shoot. It may take a long time, but seedlings draw on an amazing power to live and become trees.

Even in the light of day, we may not be aware of those forces around us that choke our growth, that make us bitter, hard of heart, crooked and wilted. We need the daily power of prayer to grow in and toward the light that is God. Prayer is not a power to remove obstacles to growth; prayer is a reliance on God that he will raise us to grow through obstacles.

The smallest of living things around us have much to teach us about ourselves, if we take the time to look at them. Many are right at our feet. Perhaps a good prayer for today would be to ask God to see and learn from the power of the small and the wisdom that is patience. Growth takes time, persistence, patience. And, yes, it moves vast things.

Fr. James Stephen Behrens, O.C.S.O.

Like Precious Jewels

> When one finds a worthy wife,
> her value is far beyond pearls.
> Her husband, entrusting his heart to her,
> has an unfailing prize. Proverbs 31:10

"What's the secret of your marriage?" my wife and I have been asked on many occasions while helping prepare young couples for married life in our parish's marriage preparation program. We talk about respect, communication and our shared faith.

As I read this Scripture passage, I realize that the "unfailing prize" of our marriage is that, on the day we wed, we entrusted our hearts to one another. Throughout our marriage, we have managed, through faith, prayer and a mutual understanding of our commitment, to daily affirm that trust. We didn't say, "Let's give it a shot and see what happens." We didn't run the course until the course got too tough. We just entrusted our hearts to one another. We're not better people than those whose marriages have failed. We're not perfect. But we have never failed to remember that we hold each other's hearts, cradled like precious jewels, never to be broken or traded.

Lord, thank you for giving us people who we can trust with our hearts.

Steve Givens

A Mother's Influence

> Jesus said to them, "Do you believe that I can do this?" "Yes, Lord," they said to him. Then he touched their eyes and said, "Let it be done for you according to your faith."
>
> Matthew 9:28-29

Jesus' words are reminiscent of Mary's fiat: "May it be done to me according to your word" (Luke 1:38). I imagine her using such phrases often as Jesus grew up in her presence. Did he pick up on her mannerisms? Did he see the faith behind the words?

Whatever knowledge his divinity might have given him, Jesus surely learned to recognize the power of faith in God at home. He had many opportunities to see that power at work: traveling with his family, talking with the elders in the synagogue, seeing his disciples leave everything to follow him.

So Jesus asked the poor and injured, "Do you believe ...?" He didn't question their motives or weigh his abilities against their afflictions. He didn't promise that their desire would be fulfilled. He simply invited them to share in his hope, a hope he had seen and lived out from his earliest days.

Jesus, your family had faith in you. May my hope be in you.

Julia DiSalvo

Trust As Mary Did

Mary said, "Behold, I am the handmaid of the Lord. May it be done to me according to your word." Luke 1:38

These words were Mary's faith-filled response to the angel's announcement of her son's miraculous birth. The angel never explained in detail how this was to take place. How do you fully explain a virgin birth? But Mary needed no detailed explanation. It was enough that the promise was made. Moved by God's grace, Mary chose to respond with loving faith to the plan God had laid out for her, a plan she did not fully understand.

We can apply Mary's experience to our lives. God promises to be with us when the events of our lives carry us beyond our ability to understand them. In those circumstances, God gives us the courage to walk with faith, and to believe that our trust in him will ultimately bring us peace of mind and heart. God will certainly give this gift to all who pray for it, for without faith, our lives can have no meaning or joy.

Lord, strengthen my faith. May I trust as Mary did, relying on your guidance to lead me over pathways I do not quite understand.

Fr. Kenneth Grabner, C.S.C.

September 29

Assessing Our Desires

Now I, in turn, give him to the Lord; as long as he lives, he shall be dedicated to the Lord. 1 Samuel 1:28

Wonderful and mysterious things happen when we are willing to hold lightly what God has given to us. Although Hannah had longed for a child, she did not cling to Samuel, but consecrates the child she had so ardently prayed for to the Lord. At the time she had no idea that Samuel would someday become a prophet through whom God would anoint David king.

It may or may not be a literal child, but each of us has something that we long for with all our hearts. It might be a position we have always wanted to hold, a creative work we have dreamed of producing or perhaps a material possession. While our desires are not bad in themselves, we can become obsessed and lose our freedom if we make this desire the center of our universe.

Hannah is a powerful model of faith as she entrusted both her prayer and the answer to God. Before you go to sleep tonight reflect on your day and notice if there is anything that began as a good desire and has grown into an unhealthy need.

Terri Mifek

WITH COURAGE AND FAITH

**Wait for the LORD with courage;
be stouthearted, and wait for the LORD.** Psalm 27:14

Many of us are not good at waiting. Due to the wonders of the Internet, we no longer need to wait in line for a bank teller, for tickets to the cinema, for take-out food or a host of other things.

When we do have to wait, especially for an answer to our prayers, we are often impatient. As we await the Lord, we are usually anxious because of the seriousness of the situation. But that's largely because we are thinking of God as a request-filler, a clerk at a counter. We take a number (say our prayers) and wait for a reply.

Waiting for the Lord with courage could mean that we are meant to cooperate with God. We pray, yes, but then we go about doing our part to help the situation. Apparently, God longs for us to work with him, to be courageous through our actions and then, patiently and with faith, wait.

Terence Hegarty

Helping Jesus With Our Prayers

She came and fell at his feet. Mark 7:25

If we turn our hearts to this gospel passage, opening our eyes and ears to the faith of this Syrophoenician woman we might learn how to pray. From her we can learn perseverance. There is no half-love sounding in her cry for help. She loves her wounded daughter. Even in the face of Jesus' seeming scorn she pushes forward with an undivided heart.

I like this woman. Her courage and boldness intrigue me. Her stubborn love captivates my heart. Oh how I need her steadfast faith. I would like to bring her single-hearted intention into all my prayer. She has become my model of prayer. I have resolved to turn my face toward this woman and learn from her. There is a spiritual power in us that can assist Jesus in answering prayer. Our love united with the love of Christ can wash over the one for whom we are praying and work wonders.

Sr. Macrina Wiederkehr, O.S.B

A Lesson in Humility

Then Jesus straightened up and said to her, "Woman, where are they? Has no one condemned you?" John 8:10

Once during an argument with my wife, she said something that helped me realize I was the one who was wrong. At first, I was so certain that I had the moral high ground and she was mistaken that it shook me to my core when I understood the gravity of my mistake. I felt embarrassed, ashamed and very vulnerable. But even at the tail end of a heated conflict, my wife backed down. She said it was all right, accepted my apology and even gave me a hug! How easily she could have laid into me for my arrogance and lack of listening skills. But she did not. And because of that, I learned much more about love, respect and humility.

The woman in the gospel story is more like us than we might want to admit: no one is immune from sin. Since we are all related in this way, our impulse should be to exercise our powers of empathy and compassion when it is apparent that others are struggling with sin, rather than assuming we are morally superior.

David Nantais

October 3

AN APRON IS A HOLY THING

He took a towel and tied it around his waist. John 13:4

After my mother died we divvied up her things. One thing I wanted badly was one of her aprons. You know the kind: large bib, long strings and at least one pocket. Now every time I don that apron, I kiss it reverently and say a little prayer for Mom. I also pray that I may serve as generously and as joyfully as she did.

An apron is a holy thing. At the Last Supper Jesus himself donned a makeshift apron when he wrapped a towel around his waist before he washed his disciples' feet. Aprons are also symbolic. They remind us that serving others is not always neat. Our various forms of loving can get messy at times.

Anytime that we commemorate the Last Supper, let our hearts be filled with gratitude—for the eucharistic banquet we celebrate, for the people who have served us throughout our life and for all those individuals for whom we don our apron.

Servant Jesus, may I serve the people in my life as generously and graciously as you did.

Sr. Melannie Svoboda, S.N.D.

Jesus Responds to 'Great Faith'

Then Jesus said to her in reply, "O woman, great is your faith! Let it be done for you as you wish." And her daughter was healed from that hour. Matthew 15:28

Jesus is confronted by a Canaanite woman, a person on the fringe of his culture on three counts: she is a woman, a non-Jew and appears to be a single mother. The disciples want Jesus to get rid of her because she is a nuisance. But when Jesus takes time to listen and dialogue with this outsider, he discovers her profound faith. In fact, in all of Matthew's Gospel, she is the only person whose faith is said to be "great."

We may sometimes judge that others who are outside our Church or culture are lacking in faith or favor with God. Or we may feel that we are on the outside, the fringe, of Church, culture, family or some socially respectable group. For Jesus, this does not matter; all that matters is our faith.

God, grant me the gift of great faith to believe that you always listen and respond to me.

Sr. Ruth Marlene Fox, O.S.B.

October 5

FORGIVING THE UNFORGIVABLE

My sacrifice, O God, is a contrite spirit;
a heart contrite and humbled, O God, you will not spurn.

Psalm 51:19

Imagine being wrapped up in sin the way David was! Not only had he bedded a valued warrior's wife, he had then sent the husband to certain death to hide the fact that David was responsible for the woman's pregnancy. It makes our own misdeeds look pretty small.

But they don't feel small, do they? When we reflect on how we have cheated and dishonored other people and the Lord himself, we can feel there's no way we can be forgiven. That fear can keep us away from the sacrament of reconciliation, from Mass, from prayer itself!

David had great faith and even the greatest of sins couldn't keep him away from God. Called out on his behavior by the prophet Nathan, the king—contrite, humbled and penitent—threw himself at the Lord's feet. The Father longs for us to have the same confidence in his love, no matter how far we have gone astray.

Lord, please accept my sacrifice, that of a contrite spirit.

Melanie Rigney

Handing Down the Faith

Our Father in heaven,
   hallowed be your name,
   your kingdom come,
   your will be done,
   on earth as it is in heaven. Matthew 6:9-10

Jesus taught his disciples to pray this prayer, which we say now together at Mass. I am fascinated by the ancestry of prayer. The week after Easter, we hear Peter in Acts 2 addressing the crowd at Pentecost in Jerusalem, quoting David's words in Psalm 16, a prophesy of Jesus' resurrection. Peter is speaking 2,000 years ago, quoting David 1,000 years before that, and we hear it now in faith community!

We say the rosary using words the Angel Gabriel said to Mary at the annunciation. And I say those words using my mother's rosary. The prayer Jesus said when he died, "Into your hands I commend my spirit" (Luke 23:46) was the ancient Psalm 31:6. Like DNA of faith passed on, I have my great-grandfather's crucifix commemorating that moment.

Jesus, help each of us to keep transmitting this precious inheritance, giving thanks for those who handed the faith on to us.

Patricia Livingston

Flight in the Night

> **During the night, the angel of the Lord opened the doors of the prison, led them out, and said, "Go and take your place in the temple area, and tell the people everything about this life."** Acts 5:19-20

When my sister was in her early twenties, she became trapped in an unhealthy relationship. Having reached a breaking point late one night, she called me for a ride. With nowhere else to go and her infant left behind, she entered my car with only her purse and a trash bag of necessities.

I hardly felt like an angel that evening, but as the family gathered and listened to her story, God's grace became more visible. Within 48 hours she was able to collect her belongings, reunite with her daughter and reach safety. As my mother recalls, she was finally willing to speak the truth and submit to God's will.

Risen Jesus, fill the hearts of your children with the power of your Spirit.

Julia DiSalvo

Treasure That Moment

How does this happen to me, that the mother of my Lord should come to me? Luke 1:43

Elizabeth has been on quite an eventful streak. First, she becomes pregnant after having all but given up on ever bearing a child. Now, filled with the Holy Spirit, she recognizes that the mother of her Lord has come to visit. How, indeed, does this happen? Scripture provides little more explanation for such events than attributing it to the power of God. And surely everything under the sun can be attributed to the power of God. For Elizabeth, filled with the Holy Spirit, this is a marvelous, exhilarating, awesome moment. As it is for Mary too.

Does every life have such moments of clear insight into the undeniable presence of God? Soon Elizabeth's days would be taken up with the routine tasks of caring for a baby and raising the child with Zechariah. I imagine that, like Mary, she "treasured all these things," stopping from time to time to marvel at all that God had done in her life. Take a moment to treasure a time in your own life when you were aware that God had come to you.

Mark Neilsen

October 9

God Has Much More to Share

I have much more to tell you, but you cannot bear it now.

John 16:12

My mother was a great one for telling sad news in installments. She might begin by mentioning that someone was ill. Then a bit later, that the same person was receiving critical care. Then that they were on life support. And finally, that they had died. I've always supposed that this was her gentle way of preparing the listener for a truth that would be overwhelming if given all at once.

On the deepest level, this seems to have been Jesus' approach with his disciples. He told them, little by little and over and over, that he was destined to be crucified and to die, but that he would not leave them orphans. He compassionately prepared them (and us) for his leave-taking with stories and parables, with his presence in the Eucharist, with the promise of the Spirit.

Jesus, let me listen for the "much more" that you have to tell me.

Sr. Chris Koellhoffer, I.H.M.

The Human Condition

Behold, the hour is coming and has arrived when each of you will be scattered to his own home and you will leave me alone. John 16:32

The day our first child left for college was a difficult one, and I couldn't help crying as I walked through her empty bedroom. Our youngest daughter who was eight at the time gave me a big hug and assured me with great conviction that she would never leave home. Of course, I knew perfectly well that one day it would be time for her to go as well, but I also knew that if I told her that, she wouldn't believe me.

Jesus was aware that things were about to become violent and that his followers would find it difficult to remain faithful to him. He also knew that people make promises based on what they know at the time. When I read this line of Scripture now I understand it differently from when I was young. I no longer hear it as an indictment of failure, but as an observation by a wise person fully aware of the human condition.

Terri Mifek

A Need for Island Time

**The Lord is king; let the earth rejoice;
let the many isles be glad.** Psalm 97:1

Of all the days of the year, October 12, which marks the birth of my oldest child, my son Luke, is perhaps my favorite. It is the anniversary of my motherhood.

The greatest transformations of my life have been my faith and my motherhood. Both have made me less selfish, more loving, more willing to sacrifice and less willing to settle for less. I am a different woman because my heart has been changed in these ways.

One of my best friends shared something with me about her marriage and why it remains so strong in such a fragile culture. She refers to her marriage, and now her family life, as their "island." Other people can visit, but they live there.

Our most sacred relationships—with God, our families, our friends—need island time. The Lord is king; let the many islands be glad.

Kristin Armstrong

Remaining Faithful

He rejoiced and encouraged them all to remain faithful to the Lord in firmness of heart... Acts 11:23

At one time I thought that visiting with the elderly was a kindness we did for them, but I realize now what a gift it is to listen to their stories. This is especially true when people are able to look back and see how God was at work in everything in their lives, even what they considered their failures.

I recently visited with a beautiful friend in her late seventies who has suffered many disappointments and heartaches in her life. As we talked she shared with me that at one time in her life she had become rather self-righteous; however, the experience of having a teenage daughter become pregnant had made her less judgmental and more compassionate. The twinkle in her eye and the openness of her heart reminded me of what we can become when we remain faithful to our deepest call to love as God loves.

Terri Mifek

Going the Extra Mile

Should anyone press you into service for one mile, go with him for two miles. Matthew 5:41

As a runner, this verse jumps off the page and straight into my heart. The women I run with are a sisterhood to me: We train hard together—physically and spiritually. I recall a day when our friend Paige arrived late to a workout. We were running a series of hill repeats, and when we finished she still had one left to do. Because we love her and didn't want her to suffer alone, we joined her for her final effort and finished strong as a group.

Even if it means going above and beyond what we originally set out to do, there are times when God calls upon us to build endurance. Instead of resisting or resenting these opportunities, we might consider that God has us in a training program. He might be refining us and building our strength so that we are ready for our next assignment. You have more to offer than you can possibly imagine. Believe him.

Kristin Armstrong

SOWING BOUNTIFULLY

Whoever sows sparingly will also reap sparingly, and whoever sows bountifully will also reap bountifully. 2 Corinthians 9:6

Long ago in 1858, Bernadette of Lourdes had a series of "visions" of a woman. On her ninth visit, that woman told Bernadette to drink from a spring. The place where she pointed was only earth; the girl dug into the earth and drank only mud, while the crowd behind, seeing her dirty face, thought her crazy. Only later, when the people had left, did the water begin to flow, and the healing waters of faith have flowed there ever since.

We may have good reason to sow sparingly. Bernadette did. She could quite reasonably have refused to follow the unknown woman's incomprehensible direction and kept her dignity. Instead she trusted and looked foolish, even insane. Her faithful response reaped incredible bounty, establishing a place of healing and sanctuary for many, for the unknown woman turned out to be the Blessed Mother. What am I afraid to let go of, rather than allow God to work his miracle of abundance?

Mary Marrocco

OCTOBER 15

The Ocean

**You have made him little less than the angels,
and crowned him with glory and honor.** Psalm 8:6

When we are in the throes of autumn, I like to reflect on the recently passed summer. Each year, at least once, I manage to get to the ocean. I simply love the first few moments of my initial visit to the seashore. As the water laps over my feet, with sand between my toes, I stand and marvel, attempting to gain some grasp of the wonder of this part of God's creation. I enjoy trying to make sense of the sheer size and complexity of this thing we call the Atlantic Ocean. And I have often felt insignificant in the face of it.

But then I consider the truth that the heavens and the earth will pass away, but we will not. Even standing in the surf with natural power and grandeur all around, I know that we—every single one of us—are each a grand, majestic and glorious creation!

Terence Hegarty

'In Her Heart'

He went down with them and came to Nazareth, and was obedient to them; and his mother kept all these things in her heart. Luke 2:51

Many of the images of Mary through the ages in religious art and devotional writing portray her as if she were on a pedestal. For me, the emphasis on her stainless perfection can obscure her very real humanness. What touches me deeply is not so much the fact that hers was an immaculate heart, but that hers was a heart that reflected, gathered and kept "all these things."

This verse, after searching and finding Jesus, was the second time Luke used the phrase she "kept all these things in her heart." The first time was in Bethlehem after the shepherds came reporting what the angels had said. She kept close within her times of stunning joy and great anxiety. I feel encouraged by her company as I hold within me poignant moments in my own life, vivid times of joy and fear, moments that are backlit by mystery. I am "heartened" by her great heart.

Patricia Livingston

Coming Home

Not only will I go down to Egypt with you; I will also bring you back here, after Joseph has closed your eyes. Genesis 46:4

My aunt was born and raised in a small, Missouri town. Her seven siblings stayed within a two-hour drive, but she left to raise her family on the East Coast. At times she longed to return home, but it would be over twenty years, widowed and with a child out of college, before she found her opportunity. On the day her new Midwestern house was scheduled to close, she passed away. We buried her near her parents, finally back in her hometown.

Canaan was Jacob's homeland. As he gathered his family and left to meet Joseph in Egypt, perhaps he wondered if he would ever return, even if after his death. God made him that promise, and he kept it.

God, thanks for staying near me wherever I go. I hope to come home to you someday.

Julia DiSalvo

In Plain Sight

Jesus said to her, "Woman, why are you weeping? Whom are you looking for?" John 20:15

He was there, right in front of her eyes, but Mary Magdalene mistook him for the gardener.

He's there, right in front of our eyes too. Sometimes he's easy to see: in our pastor's homily, perhaps, or in a child's smile. It's harder to see him in the street person who asks if we have any spare change or the friend who asks us to go with her to a doctor's appointment at a time that's inconvenient. But then, Jesus never promised us that following him would be easy. He did promise that he'd be with us always, right by our side. And when we remember that, we find him everywhere.

Jesus, help me to recognize you in all the forms you appear to me each day.

Melanie Rigney

Knowing His Presence

Having come down in a cloud, the Lord stood with him there... Moses at once bowed down to the ground in worship.

Exodus 34:5, 8

My youngest daughter, not yet school age, is not too sure about Santa. Although a few presents appear on Christmas morning without a giver's name attached, we rarely talk about him. Even when we occasionally see a man in a red suit during the holidays, she invariably points and cries, "There's somebody dressed as Santa!"

She's not too sure about God, either. She asks sometimes if he's real. For all my ambivalence about Santa, I answer her questions about God emphatically. We talk about the intangible, mystical presence of God. We pray together at home and at church. It would be helpful if God came to us in a concrete and physical way, like the cloud that appeared to Moses. But until that happens, we say that God is the love we experience in the world—like our love for each other. She knows that is real.

Loving God, may we know your presence.

Karla Manternach

Even Now

Martha said to Jesus, "Lord, if you had been here, my brother would not have died. [But] even now I know that whatever you ask of God, God will give you." John 11:21-22

Martha's emotions and faith are right up-front: On the one hand, she seems to be scolding Jesus for his absence, and on the other, she is steadfast and unshaken in declaring her belief in Jesus' power to heal—even at this late date.

Her words are consoling to any of us who struggle with the dark night of the soul, who live through periods in our lives when God seems distant if not totally out of the picture, who feel as if our pleas for ourselves or those we love seem completely forgotten by God.

At those times, let our prayer echo that of outspoken Martha: Even now I know. Even now I believe.

Sr. Chris Koellhoffer, I.H.M.

HIS UNEXPECTED WAYS

> **Then Jesus said to her in reply, "O woman, great is your faith! Let it be done for you as you wish." And her daughter was healed from that hour.** Matthew 15:28

Because the exchange between Jesus and the Canaanite woman is familiar, we may easily miss how shocking it was to the Jewish Christians who first heard it. As a Canaanite, this woman was a Gentile. Even spoken kindly, Jesus' words constitute a verbal slap in the face.

But the woman is not put off. She continues to address him as "Lord." She continues to believe that he can help her afflicted daughter. She even accepts Jesus' "dog" metaphor and uses it to her own advantage, being so bold as to become Jesus' teacher. She politely explains to him the nature of true mercy. Far from being offended, Jesus is impressed with the woman's words as indicative of true faith.

Mitch Finley

In Ministry Together

Accompanying him were the Twelve and some women...

Luke 8:1-2

I taught seminarians pastoral theology, that is, how to minister in a pastoral setting. At some point, I would ask them, "Do you feel comfortable working with women? I hope so, because the majority of the people who will work in your parish will be women."

Women have, and have always had, a major role in the Church. Jesus was accompanied by the Twelve and also by a group of women. Three are named—Mary Magdalene, Susanna and Joanna—and there were "many others." The Scriptures imply that there were a lot of women, perhaps more numerous than the men.

Following Jesus' example, women and men have been ministering together in the Church for over two millennia. Each of us in the Church ought to challenge ourselves by asking, *How comfortable am I working with the other gender?*

Msgr. Stephen J. Rossetti

SEEN, HEALED

When Jesus saw her, he called her and said, "Woman, you are set free of your infirmity." He laid his hands on her, and she at once stood up straight and glorified God. Luke 13:12-13

She appears when needed, a wise nun told me. This unnamed woman, one of the little ones of Luke's Gospel, speaking no words at all, is easily overlooked. She merely shows up at a Sabbath service one day, as she's done regularly for 18 years. She's unable to look people in the eye—bent double by an infirmity—and chances are, people don't see her at all. Except Jesus does. We don't know, but can readily imagine, her suffering. Likewise, what it took for her to receive his loving touch and allow herself to become what she was meant to be. This is her greatness. By receiving freedom from Christ's touch, she gave glory to God.

What is it that bends me down to the ground and makes me unable to see or to be seen by others as I really am? Guided by this splendid woman, let us learn to let go of our burdens and glorify God by becoming whole.

Woman of God, help me to receive the touch that brings healing and wholeness.

Mary Marrocco

God's Maternal Side

Blessed is the womb that carried you... Luke 11:27

One could certainly be a fine Christian and not have a devotion to the Blessed Virgin Mary. But would something be missing?

When Pope Benedict reflected on this question, he responded, "Our first attempt at an answer could be his [God's] maternal side, which reveals itself more purely and more directly in the Son's mother than anywhere else." Mary reminds us of the nurturing, compassionate maternity of God.

It is difficult at times to think of our all-powerful Creator in terms of a loving Mother who nurtures us into life. Mary helps us to do that.

If our modern world has lost touch with its Maker, part of the problem may be its lack of awareness of who this loving Creator really us. Mary can be an answer especially for those who long to be cradled in the loving arms of a beautiful Mother.

Msgr. Stephen J. Rossetti

An Unshakable Faith

Mary said, "Behold, I am the handmaid of the Lord. May it be done to me according to your word." Luke 1:38

Of all the beautiful things Mary ever said, this is my favorite. I have memorized it, and I pray it back to God whenever I feel the pinch of adversity.

Can you imagine how scared she must have been? A young virgin, engaged to be married, visited by an angel who tells her that she will bear God's son. If I were in that situation, I would likely have fainted outright or come back with a million questions. *How is that going to work, exactly? And what am I supposed to tell Joseph? My family is not going to be too thrilled about this. What if no one believes me?*

But our beloved Mary did not respond in such a faithless, feeble way. She was unshakable. And that is precisely why God chose her. I long to have faith like that—to say, simply, "May it be done to me according to your word."

Kristin Armstrong

TO BE HUNGRY?

I do not want to send them away hungry, for fear they may collapse on the way. Matthew 15:32

Go away hungry? With school festivities, office gatherings, brunches, parties and other get-togethers, it seems like we eat and drink nonstop. Hunger is the last thing we have to worry about... or is it?

Remember that, while Jesus fed the crowd physically with those loaves and fishes, he also satisfied their hunger in a deeper, spiritual way. As the ideal host, he does the same for us when we tarry a while at his table, drinking in his wisdom, being nourished by his love.

If we can commit to an extra five or ten minutes in prayer or meditation to start or end our day, we will find ourselves spiritually and mentally fortified—and ready to help feed those who most need it.

Jesus, I thank you for the banquet you set before me every day.

Melanie Rigney

God Stands by Us

Fear not, O worm Jacob,
  O maggot Israel;
I will help you, says the Lord. Isaiah 41:14

I had been jumping on the bed again. I'd already broken the box spring once. Now I'd done it again. My mother was so angry she wouldn't speak to me, so I wrote her a letter. I said how sorry I was. I asked for forgiveness. I still have the note she wrote back: "Violets are blue. Roses are red. I love you even with a broken bed." She didn't fix my bed (again) for a while. But her note was all I needed. I knew then that, angry as she was, she still loved me, no matter what I had done.

The people of Israel repeatedly broke the promises they made to God. He had every reason to be fed up, and in the passage above, it sounds like he was! But it also sounds like he was prepared to stand by them anyway. He does this for us, too, no matter how many times we fail.

Gracious God, I turn to you, trusting in your love for me.

Karla Manternach

TEACH US THE WAY

**Guide me in your truth and teach me,
for you are God my savior.** Psalm 25:5

Last year I received a Christmas card from a friend saying she had experienced a "challenging" year. She stated her faith had been tested in many ways regarding what is true and moral. I suspect most of us have similar feelings. We hear various views openly discussed today that are contrary to what we have been taught. In our efforts to obtain genuine wisdom, we can imitate the ancient psalmist who prayerfully begged God to guide him in the truth and teach him the correct way to think and act. Often we will need to reject the opinions of the world, and other times we may need to revise some of our past views as we grow in understanding. The difficulty is in knowing what to avoid and what to revise. The psalmist also says God will teach the humble his way. If we turn to God in prayer with a trustful, sincere and humble attitude, the Lord has promised to lead us to the truth.

Speak Lord, your servant is listening.

Fr. James McKarns

Having an Open and Humble Heart

Amen I say to you, tax collectors and prostitutes are entering the kingdom of God before you. Matthew 21:31

We make assumptions about people and are taken back when they don't follow the script we have written for them. This is most evident to me as I think of our grown daughters. The daughter who once loved big city living on the east coast eventually settled in rural Minnesota while the daughter who disliked school earned an advanced degree. A third daughter whose whole life was centered on academics became a fitness enthusiast in her thirties.

People surprise us, and if we are wise we will allow God to be God and that means we must be open to new ways of seeing. Who would have guessed that God would come hidden as a tiny, helpless infant or that God is evidently more interested in an open and humble heart than a list of our virtues?

Loving Creator, your vision is beyond our understanding open our eyes to the wonders of your love.

Terri Mifek

Finding New Words for Prayer

Sing to the LORD a new song,
    for he has done wondrous deeds. Psalm 98:1

Have you ever said about someone, "She keeps singing the same old song"? It means, of course, that a certain pattern of thought is repeated over and over, like the refrain of a familiar—and boring—song. Probably the people who know me best could also recognize my customary songs: "I am so busy." "Sorry, I don't have time to help you."

What is the same old song that you like to sing at home and work? More importantly, what is the theme of your song to God every day? This psalm suggests that we sing a new song to God, that we try a new refrain. Perhaps instead of "Please give me," I might try, "Thanks for everything." It would be an interesting experiment to see how many new phrases I could use in my prayers. I might surprise myself and God with some fresh, creative and inspiring prayers.

Sr. Ruth Marlene Fox, O.S.B.

October 31

Saints: Beatitude People

**Blessed are the poor in spirit,
for theirs is the kingdom of heaven.** Matthew 5:3

Sainthood can be easily dismissed as an impossible lifestyle far beyond our reach. After all, most of us do not wear sackcloth, pray ten hours a day, start a religious congregation or risk being fed to lions. So, we're off the hook, yes?

No. For the Beatitudes give us a portrait of a saint that is more attainable than we might think. Saints can be poor by worldly standards, mostly because they share generously what they have with others. Saints can mourn without despairing. They deal with others gently rather than violently. Saints can withstand insult and injury. They forgive others their failings. Saints hunger for a better world. They are never completely satisfied. Rather, they live St. Augustine's words: "My soul is restless, O Lord, until it rests in Thee."

Does the above description remind you of anyone? And do you find any traces of yourself in the Beatitudes?

Jesus, you lived the Beatitudes. Help me to become more and more a Beatitude person.

Sr. Melannie Svoboda, S.N.D.

Claimed by Christ

For this is the will of my Father, that everyone who sees the Son and believes in him may have eternal life, and I shall raise him [on] the last day. John 6:40

The white cloth draped over a casket at a funeral is meant to call to mind our baptism. At our death, just as at our baptism, a white garment symbolizes our new life in Christ. I find it astonishing and beautiful to make this connection at a time of sorrow. Even while we mourn, we remember the full circle of life and strike a chord of confidence and hope.

All Souls' Day is another occasion to make this connection. Perhaps in some part of ourselves we forever mourn the loss of a loved one. All Souls' Day is an opportunity to bring that loss to the fore. But it is also an expression of our hope and confidence that our loved ones, in death, somehow remain with us. All of us, living and dead, are claimed by Christ. We are part of a community of believers, a community that encompasses all those who have followed Christ, past and present. Through birth, life, death, rebirth and new life, we belong to one another. We belong to Christ.

Lord Jesus, grasp hold of us all!

Karla Manternach

FORGIVING OURSELVES

> [Jesus said to his disciples,] "...if you bring your gift to the altar, and there recall that your brother has anything against you, leave your gift there at the altar, go first and be reconciled with your brother, and then come and offer your gift."
>
> Matthew 5:23-24

We cannot separate our relationships with other people from our relationship with God. Oh, we can do it, all right. But if we do, we need to understand that we're shooting ourselves in the foot, spiritually speaking. Better to accept that Jesus knows what he's talking about and try to live accordingly.

It's good to remember this when we approach the sacrament of reconciliation. We want God's forgiveness, of course. But if we want reconciliation with God, we need to do what we can to be reconciled with those our sins have hurt or with the earth our sins have damaged or—and this can be the most difficult of all—often we need to forgive ourselves at the same time as we seek God's forgiveness. Frequently my sins hurt me in some way, and that automatically hurts my relationship with God.

Lord Jesus, help me to always think of others, and myself, when I think of you.

Mitch Finley

BURDENS LIFTED

Today you are making this agreement with the LORD: he is to be your God and you are to walk in his ways...

Deuteronomy 26:17

I recently sold a house I'd had on the market for a year, and the relief I feel is pretty amazing. It also surprised me: It's almost as though the worry of the extra cost and worry about the property had become so deeply ingrained, I'd forgotten that it was even a possibility that someday the burden would be lifted. I'd come to assume, deep down, that I would live with the burden forever.

My agreement with the Lord to walk more closely in his ways is sometimes a bit of a struggle. What I've given up, what I've taken on...well, I'm already arguing with myself, suggesting that keeping my end of the agreement is not really necessary. It's the spirit of the law, right? But I'll keep on because I know that some small burden of sin and attachment will be lifted, something I might not even have realized was imprisoning me, so deeply ingrained and assumed, is suddenly gone, and I'm free.

Lord, lead me to freedom on this journey.

Amy Welborn

MY WAY OR...

Stop judging and you will not be judged. Stop condemning and you will not be condemned. Luke 6:37

"Because I'm the parent." "Because I'm the boss." "Because I've been there." In so many situations, we attempt to shut down arguments with words like these, all of which amount to: "Because I'm right, case closed, end of discussion."

How merciful is God to listen to us until we run out of steam, until we realize his way is best despite all our protestations and arguments to the contrary. Perhaps we can learn from that in reconciling our relationships here on earth as well—by listening rather than judging, by loving instead of condemning. We may find our friends and family—and ourselves, in the process—drawing closer to God when we leave the pronouncements to him.

Lord, I pledge to let you do the judging and to join you as best I can in the loving.

Melanie Rigney

CLOSE AT HAND

The Lord is close to the brokenhearted. Psalm 34:19

Some of the most difficult parenting times for my wife and I were those moments when our teenaged children went through relationship breakups. We could usually see these coming, and we knew someone's heart was going to be broken. We also knew the pain would pass with time, but at the moment all we could do was to hold them and make sure they felt loved.

With each death, each divorce, each fractured relationship, our hearts are broken open as the cost and consequence of loving and trusting. We only grieve what we love and long for, and it is precisely at these moments that we find God, as close to us as our breath. We discover God at the center of our broken hearts, never promising that it won't happen again, but reassuring us we will never be alone. In the dark, sometimes lonely days of Lent, this is exactly what we long for—God, close at hand.

Loving God, be near me when I hurt most.

Steve Givens

November 6

A Faith Strengthener

> I love you, O Lord, my strength…
> My God, my rock of refuge,
>   my shield, the horn of my salvation, my stronghold!
> Praised be the Lord, I exclaim,
>   and I am safe from my enemies. Psalm 18:2-4

In this passage, we can hear the palpable delight of the psalmist. His gratitude and love cannot be contained. I have had those kinds of moments with God where I exhale the breath I have been holding and say thank you, thank you, thank you. In those moments, I know without a doubt I have been saved and redeemed.

I keep a prayer journal. On occasion, I read it and smile over my requests. Some seem small with the perspective of time. Others, yet unfulfilled, still make me ache. Some are mystifying, seeing how God worked a solution that I could never have imagined. It isn't enough to simply make petitions without thanking God for his answers. So now I also keep a gratitude journal. On these pages, I record my own psalms of wonder and thanksgiving. There is no better faith strengthener than the reminder of God's help in the past.

Kristin Armstrong

COURAGE IN FEARFUL TIMES

When they had rowed about three or four miles, they saw Jesus walking on the sea and coming near the boat, and they began to be afraid. But he said to them, "It is I. Do not be afraid." John 6:19-20

St. Catherine of Siena lived during tumultuous times, but she never let fear slow her down. The Black Death raged in Europe, mercenary armies prowled the countryside. The pope cowered in Avignon, France, leaving the administration of the Church in the hands of corrupt legates. In many ways, it was the worst of times.

But Catherine did not bemoan her fate. She did not say, "If only the Black Death would go away, if only we had perfect Church leaders, then I could really live my Christian faith." No, she became a great saint by accepting her times as the context in which God was calling her to respond and live her faith. She did not run away from the critical issues of her day. She engaged fully. We are called to do the same, knowing that Jesus walks with us, saying, "It is I. Do not be afraid."

Loving God, give me the faith, courage, wisdom, spunk and compassion of St. Catherine.

Sr. Melannie Svoboda, S.N.D.

OPEN TO HIS WILL

[After the man, Adam, had eaten of the tree,] the Lᴏʀᴅ God then called to the man and asked him, "Where are you?" He answered, "I heard you in the garden; but I was afraid, because I was naked, so I hid myself." Genesis 3:9-10

It is a truism among parents or anyone with small children that silence is really not golden at all. Silence, as a matter of fact, is an almost sure sign of trouble. We don't effortlessly grow out of that temptation, either. As was the case from the beginning of the human story, I've noticed in my own life that a sure sign that not all is well, spiritually, is my attitude to prayer. Or, to put it another way, if I find myself excusing a lazy prayer life or finding it easy to shrug off attendance at daily Mass when there's absolutely no inconvenience involved, I just might want to ask myself...what am I hiding?

Mary's example shows me another way: to set fear aside, be honest about myself, trust, welcome God's presence, be open to his will and joyfully respond, "Yes."

Holy Mary, Mother of God, pray for us sinners.

Amy Welborn

Showing Up

Which of the two did his father's will? Matthew 21:31

This is the parable of two sons. A father asks his sons to go and work in the vineyard. One son says no, but then later changes his mind and shows up. The other son immediately says "yes, sir," but then never goes to work.

This parable is an example of the way that God looks at our hearts to determine the depth of our faithfulness. It is one thing to make a bold statement about our obedience, another thing entirely to willingly and wholeheartedly comply. This story clarifies that God cares more about our actions and choices than he does about our words. He cares more about the congruence between our intentions and our integrity.

Consider today any "lame yes" you may have given God, any half-hearted compliance that has yielded the equivalent of a spiritual shrug. He sees us more deeply than that, straight through to the core of our conviction. A real yes entails showing up—in the vineyards, at the office, in our marriages, for our families, in the church pews and in acts of service.

Kristin Armstrong

November 10

Waiting in Hope

> Thus the total number of generations from Abraham to David is fourteen generations; from David to the Babylonian exile, fourteen generations; from the Babylonian exile to the Messiah, fourteen generations. Matthew 1:17

My maternal grandmother was born in France, so before traveling there, I did a little digging into my genealogy. The story I unearthed included some interesting and unexpected twists and turns, including acts of incredible generosity and commitment by some as well as some questionable choices by others. In the end, I realized how all those people making all those choices somehow contributed to where I was born and even what I would value.

As we draw closer to Christmas, we are reminded that Jesus, too, had human ancestors whose history included high and low points. God used it all to bring about the birth of Jesus, and God can use everything to bring about our transformation.

Like Mary, I often don't know what the twists and turns in my life mean, but it makes it possible to wait in hope when I simply trust that good can come out of anything.

Terri Mifek

LESSEN IN ANGER

You have heard that it was said to your ancestors, "You shall not kill; and whoever kills will be liable to judgment." But I say to you, whoever is angry with his brother will be liable to judgment... Matthew 5:21-22

I was angry at a friend recently. I didn't act on it. I didn't so much as frown in the face of my "enemy." But my anger festered like a wound. It ate at me for months. Finally, I started praying about it. I prayed to see things from my friend's point of view. I asked for help remembering that God loves us both. Only then did my anger begin to ebb.

Forgiveness is hard work. Try as we might, we can only get ourselves part way there. After that, we have to surrender ourselves to God's love and mercy. We have to be willing to lay down our anger once and for all and to let the Lord carry us the rest of the way there.

Loving God, help me to give my anger over to you and to forgive whom I need to forgive.

Karla Manternach

A Heart for the Needy

...their inheritance lasts forever. Psalm 37:18

As an Italian-American child growing up in Chicago, I could only pretend to be Irish at the annual St. Patrick's Day parade. But no pretending was necessary when celebrating the first Italian-American saint, St. Frances Xavier Cabrini! Born sickly and the youngest of 13 children, missionary dreams filled her head from childhood. Geography was her favorite subject and China her goal!

After years filled with hardship, sickness and rejection by religious orders, her dreams were realized when she founded her own order and was sent, not to China, but to America where Italian immigration had created an immense need for help of all kinds. By her death in 1917, Mother Cabrini had established schools, orphanages and hospitals throughout the Americas. The name Cabrini is still synonymous with the poor she loved so much and served so unselfishly. And she remains a source of ethnic pride for Italian-Americans.

"Give me a heart as big as the universe," she wrote. Mother Cabrini had just that.

Nadia Weer

SERVING THE LORD

...whoever wishes to be great among you shall be your servant. Matthew 20:26

It took me many years to realize that most of us are, actually, servants most of the time. We serve our families, our employers, our communities and our parishes. Everyone does much more uncompensated work than we realize.

Perhaps we need to step back and recognize this about ourselves and each other. We all hear rants about how "those people" (and every group is "those people" to some other group) are taking advantage...of us, of the system, of good fortune, of the bad fortune of others...the list is endless.

But watch people. Watch the pharmacist standing all day to fill prescriptions, the janitor cleaning winter muck from the entry way again, the person helping an elderly parent journey slowly through the grocery store. People really do want to make a contribution and work at making the world a better place. Once I started seeing this, seeing all the little services people do for each other, I found myself living closer to the kingdom of God.

Aileen O'Donoghue

Jesus: Lifelong Learner

And Jesus advanced in wisdom and age and favor before God and man. Luke 2:52

I love the image of the 12-year-old boy Jesus sitting in the Temple listening to the teachers and asking them questions. He is very eager to learn. With his curiosity and sense of wonder, he is every teacher's dream student. But Jesus' learning didn't stop when his childhood ended. He kept learning, especially from his wise carpenter father and his talented and devoted mother. Early in his public ministry, Jesus gives evidence of his vast learning, primarily through the stories he tells, the images he uses, the counsel he bestows and the conviction with which he speaks.

What about us? Are we, like Jesus, life-long learners? Have we retained our curiosity about life and our sense of wonder for the mystery of existence? Do we take time to ponder our experiences, to ask good questions and to engage in conversation with others—especially those different from ourselves?

Jesus, you were a life-long learner. Help me to be eager to learn too. Help me to be a good listener. Give me the courage to ask tough questions and the compassion to ask loving ones.

Sr. Melannie Svoboda, S.N.D.

INHERITANCE OF FORGIVENESS

> Who is there like you, the God who removes guilt
>   and pardons sin for the remnant of his inheritance;
> Who does not persist in anger forever,
>   but delights rather in clemency... Micah 7:18

My mother teases my siblings and me that she will have nothing to give us upon her death, for she is spending our inheritance each day she lives. Yet nothing could be farther from the truth. The inheritance she leaves is one of kindness to her children. With each passing day, remembrances of past wrongs and petty hurts fade away into forgetfulness, so that all that remains is love. As each of us ages, may we become more and more like our all-knowing, all-forgiving God.

Claire J. King

November 16

Who, Me?

> **Listen to my voice; then I will be your God and you shall be my people. Walk in all the ways that I command you, so that you may prosper.** Jeremiah 7:23

The wealthy Drexel family was devoted to helping those in need. Katharine's father shared his money with a number of organizations, and her stepmother provided food, clothing and other assistance to the poor. Small wonder that with these examples, Katharine in her early teens thought about becoming a sister. But she decided she couldn't bear the poverty and lack of privacy.

God, however, had other plans. When Katharine asked Pope Leo XIII to send help to the Native Americans, he instead suggested she become a missionary herself. Eventually, she said yes, and she spent decades helping thousands of people and lived as they did. Her story reminds us that obedience to the Lord's call can push us out of our comfort zone, but ultimately is the course to true happiness.

Lord, open my heart and my soul so that I may always walk in your way.

Melanie Rigney

A Storied Past

While he was still a long way off, his father caught sight of him, and was filled with compassion. He ran to his son, embraced him and kissed him. Luke 15:20

Every so often, the world—or at least tiny corners of it—is rocked by the death of a television character. The Internet explodes, tears might even be shed. It's easy to be caught up in that kind of moment, even if you look back on it later and wonder what in the world got into you, caring that much about a fictional creation. It's kind of strange, but the audiences of Romeo and Juliet through the centuries would tell us that this reaction is really nothing new.

So here, too, Jesus sketches a scene, introduces characters and draws us in. Here, in a dynamic both so clear and yet a little ambiguous, we encounter a powerful truth about ourselves, our journeys and our world. We are drawn in to contemplate our pride, our sin and our stubborn distance.

And finally, we encounter this most merciful, loving Father—and perhaps, immersed in the story that has become our own, we, too, weep—in gratitude and in joy.

Merciful Father, I enter in Jesus' story, trusting in the power of your forgiveness.

Amy Welborn

Faith in God's Plan

And Mary said: "My soul proclaims the greatness of the Lord; my spirit rejoices in God my savior." Luke 1:46-47

Even though she had long wanted a child, after a young friend of mine became pregnant, she began to wonder whether she would really love the child she was carrying and enjoy being a mother. Her anxiety seemed unfounded to her husband and family as she had always been a wonderful aunt to her nieces and nephews, but her doubts persisted despite all attempts to reassure her.

Now as I watch her thoroughly delight in her baby daughter, I think of all the times in life when we are hesitant to take a leap of faith into an unknown future. As Christmas approaches, the powerful words of Mary's Magnificat remind us of the joy we experience when we listen to our deepest desires and cooperate with a power far greater than our fears. Like Mary, our yes to God is rooted in a trust in the absolute goodness and fidelity of God rather than in a certainty that things will be easy or without any suffering.

Terri Mifek

THE VOICE OF TRUTH

For this I was born and for this I came into the world, to testify to the truth. Everyone who belongs to the truth listens to my voice. John 18:37

I want to seek the truth, to know the truth, to cherish the truth, to live the truth. I want—at least I think I want—to "belong to the truth." And in a general way, I believe that I do belong to the truth.

But if I ask whether or not I have the necessary discipline to reach that goal to the extent I am called to do and to the extent that I say I want, I have reason to pause and hang my head.

I confess, Jesus, that I don't spend nearly enough time listening to your voice. May I learn to listen to your voice in nature. May I learn to listen to your word in sacred Scripture. May I learn to listen to your messages that come to me in the celebration of Mass and reception of the sacraments. May I learn to listen more attentively to your voice in prayer.

Help me to learn the prayer of listening to your truth and to live the life of listening to your truth.

James E. Adams

Good Evening

At dawn let me hear of your kindness,
for in you I trust.
Show me the way in which I should walk,
for to you I lift up my soul. Psalm 143:8

If you're familiar with Alfred Hitchcock's movies, you know that they often center on an ordinary person caught up in shenanigans. People going about their business stumble upon events and end up, not only saving their own skin, but righting a greater wrong in the process. It's an appealing scenario because I think it reflects, albeit in more extreme terms, much of what we experience every day. We walk out the door and, right away, we're plunged into life—our actions matter, our interactions have an impact. Our actions matter in the grocery store line, in that work meeting, with family, friends and strangers. I, hopefully, won't end the day running from airplanes or hanging from a cliff, but everything I've done today will indeed have an impact—letting Jesus love through me. I'll do my best to make sure it's for the good.

Amy Welborn

FROM THE HEART OF THE MATTER

All who heard it were amazed by what had been told them by the shepherds. And Mary kept all these things, reflecting on them in her heart. Luke 2:18-19

Mary is often regarded as the first Christian contemplative because she reflected on the most amazing things "in her heart." Like many of us, I do a great deal of reflecting in my brain. That is, I strive to understand, work through solutions to problems and take prudent steps to avoid difficulties in the future. As valuable as these approaches may be in handling problems, they are of less use in dealing with mysteries.

Mary is more than a good example of confronting the mysteries of faith with one's heart as well as one's head. On earth, she asked good questions. She made reasonable requests. She remained steadfast in her trials. Now she intercedes for us, accompanies us in prayer and encourages us to seek wisdom as well as knowledge. On this first day of another new year, I can think of no better prayer than that I should become more like Mary.

O Mary conceived without sin, pray for us who have recourse to you.

Mark Neilsen

Mary, Faithful Mother at Calvary

Behold, your mother. John 19:27

No healthy person likes to suffer. Perhaps just as bad as physical suffering is the thought of suffering alone. Perhaps that explains the growth of support groups for people who are undergoing difficulties. These groups, by enlisting the presence and support of others, can be positive ways of enduring hard times. The image of Jesus on the cross is meant to tell us that God, too, understands our suffering. Like Jesus, we may feel abandoned by God during our darkest hour, but we are never really abandoned. God supports us and endures the crosses of our lives with us.

But the Christian life offers us yet another consolation in our suffering. In this gospel, we hear Jesus giving us, in the person of John, Mary to be our mother, "Behold, your mother." In that act, Mary became the mother of all.

Just as Jesus was not abandoned on the cross by his mother, so neither are we abandoned by her. As Mary faithfully kneels at the foot of Jesus' cross, so does she stay close to us in our need. "Our Lady of Sorrows" is a sure support during the calvary of our lives.

Msgr. Stephen J. Rossetti

Jesus' Inner Hen

Jerusalem, Jerusalem, you who kill the prophets and stone those sent to you... Luke 13:34

You don't have to be a mother to be a woman. Even Jesus showed his maternal instincts when he cried over the barrenness of Jerusalem: "How many times I yearned to gather your children together as a hen gathers her brood under her wings, but you were unwilling!" (Luke 13:34). In another place, he called himself the bridegroom, and St. Paul, of course, called this the "great mystery," Christ and his bride the Church, their marriage consummated on the cross (Ephesians 5:32). The last image of the Bible is the wedding of the Lamb, the new Genesis fulfilling the original promise of Creation. So, relationships form our very selves, especially as Christians. Fruitful relationships they have to be! Could be "children," but they make a mother of us all!

Miguel Dulick

Mary Was a Believer

Blessed are you who believed that what was spoken to you by the Lord would be fulfilled. Luke 1:45

Over the centuries the Church has given Mary many beautiful titles: Mother of God, Blessed Virgin, Our Lady, Queen of Heaven, Mother of the Church, to name a few. But Elizabeth gives Mary perhaps her most significant title: Believer. To say Mary was a believer means she didn't know everything or have all the answers. When she said her "yes" to God to become the mother of Jesus, she didn't know what the future would hold for her and her child. In other words, she didn't know the full consequences of her yes to God. But Mary didn't need to know everything, because she believed in God. More than that, she trusted that God would be with her every step of the way. And that trust was all God needed to work marvels in and through her.

What about us? Are we true believers? Like Mary do we trust that God is with us no matter what may happen in our lives? Mary, my fellow believer, help me to trust God—no matter what.

Sr. Melannie Svoboda, S.N.D.

THE HUMILITY TO ASK

Ask and it will be given to you. Matthew 7:7

One sunny summer day our young neighbors packed up their four children and abandoned the house they had called home for nearly a decade. It was only later that we learned that they had lost their home because a balloon payment had come due and they couldn't make the payment. "If only they had told us they were in financial trouble we would have been happy and able to help them out." "Why didn't they let us know what was happening so we could support them?" These were among the bewildered responses of the friends they left behind.

We are taught from an early age that it is good to be powerful and in control; vulnerability is not something held up as desirable. No wonder many of us find it difficult to ask for help. It is only when I take time in prayer to listen to what is really going on in my heart and mind that I find the humility to acknowledge my dependence on God and ask for what I truthfully need.

Terri Mifek

Giving All

> [Jesus] said, "I tell you truly, this poor widow put in more than all the rest; for those others have all made offerings from their surplus wealth, but she, from her poverty, has offered her whole livelihood." Luke 21:3-4

We can imagine this widow clutching those two small coins together. Perhaps her palm was sweating with anxiety as she thought of other necessities that this pittance might buy—a few measures of flour, a few ounces of oil to feed her children.

How difficult her life must have been, turned upside down by the death of her husband, the loss of whom made her one of the invisible ones, counting for little in the social world of her time.

We're not told how she managed to survive. What we do know is that her quiet witness spoke eloquently of her deep trust in a provident God. Those two coins were all she had to offer, but they were everything.

Sr. Chris Koellhoffer, I.H.M.

Change and Growth

O, that today you would hear his voice. Psalm 95:7

The other day I went for my annual checkup and learned that despite taking medication, exercising daily and watching what I eat my cholesterol levels are still not at an optimal level. Much to my dismay even losing ten pounds didn't do much to improve the numbers. The doctor could see I was discouraged and said, "Don't beat yourself up. With your genetics you are doing an awesome job." His words were music to my ears and gave me the incentive to continue doing what I can to stay healthy.

We all have places in our hearts that need to be restored to health. While taking an honest inventory of the state of our spiritual health is good and necessary, it is vital to balance our desire for transformation with patience and kindness. The voice of the Holy One encourages us to change and grow but never uses shame to bully us into perfection.

Terri Mifek

Our Unique Road to Sanctity

...let us strive to know the Lord. Hosea 6:3

St. Frances of Rome was born into a wealthy family in the 14th century. Her family planned an arranged marriage when she was 12. She desperately wanted to enter religious life and cried out to God for relief. Her confessor confronted her, "Are you crying because you want to do God's will or because you want God to do your will?"

Frances married and remained happily so for 40 years. Throughout her marriage, she led a devout life, attending Mass, visiting the sick and helping the poor. After her husband's death, she was finally able to enter religious life.

At times, we find ourselves in unwanted situations. We, too, are tempted to cry out for relief. But this path may be an essential part of our way to holiness. Let us pray, then, for the courage to follow God's will. May we follow our own God-given and unique road to sanctity.

Msgr. Stephen J. Rossetti

Stay Open to Those Around You

Then God opened her eyes, and she saw a well of water.

Genesis 21:19

Let these few lines from the Book of Genesis lead you through this day. Walk with wide open eyes. Watch for hidden wells along the way. Be especially attentive to the wellsprings of your own heart. You may be the angel God chooses to lead others to a well.

Does your heart not go out to Hagar in the wilderness? Imagine her lonely flight into the wastelands. Rejected and driven away by Sarah and Abraham, she feels desolate, forsaken. How miserable she must be to abandon her own child and wait for death! But God hears the child's cry and sends an angel. Watch for Hagar today. She may be in your own household, feeling lonely and rejected. Listen to her child crying to be fed and comforted. Open your eyes wide. Who is she?

And what about the "Hagar" in you? Who is the angel from heaven who has opened your eyes? Where are your wells?

Lord, may my prayer and devotion serve to open my heart to all those around me.

Sr. Macrina Wiederkehr, O.S.B.

A FAITH JESUS COULD NOT RESIST

Courage, daughter! Your faith has saved you. Matthew 9:22

This woman who had been hemorrhaging for 12 years had the courage to break all kinds of taboos and believe that Jesus would respond. She believed God's Messiah would not be bound by human conventions, no matter how permanent and unbreakable they seemed. Her faith was so much bigger than obedience to religious conventions. She showed that faith is embracing a personal God with all of one's being. What courage this takes, especially when it's a leap into uncharted waters!

Jesus responded to this faith—immediately and compassionately. The woman was considered unclean and so a sinner. She was excluded from the community and from worship in the Temple. But Jesus praised her faith and courage and healed her. As followers of Jesus, we are being asked to respond with similar compassion to those considered unclean in our own time.

Jesus, help us learn from this daughter of God to be both courageous and compassionate on behalf of people crying out for healing acceptance.

James McGinnis

DISCERNMENT

Jesus, tired from his journey, sat down there at the well.

John 4:6

How many times has it happened to us? A day at work so difficult we're totally enervated; a conversation so uncomfortable we simply can't wait for it to be over; a highly charged confrontation that robs us of every ounce of physical and psychic energy. All we long for at such times is a place of quiet, a place apart, a place where we can be alone and restored. And sometimes that's exactly the time, when our energy has left us, that there's a knock on the door, an unexpected visitor or someone needing our total attention.

Jesus was tired, and he sat down by himself. I suspect he was looking forward to a chance to recharge and be renewed. And yet, something about the Samaritan woman led him to draw her into conversation—and what a conversation it was!

May we, as Jesus did, clearly discern and balance our own needs and the needs of our neighbor.

Sr. Chris Koellhoffer, I.H.M.

The Reality of Rescue

When you pass through the water, I will be with you;
in the rivers you shall not drown.
When you walk through fire, you shall not be burned;
the flames shall not consume you. Isaiah 43:2

Many of life's crises have the power of a raging river, sweeping us off our feet and into a whirlpool of doubt and distress. Sometimes, we may land in a situation that explodes like fire with anger or emotional pain. I've been stunned by such occurrences, so much so that I have had difficulty in knowing how to ask for God's help. The feeling of helplessness can be overwhelming. Then, a kind word from a friend or an offer from a stranger who promises to pray for me, bring me back to an awareness that I am not alone in my heartache or grief. God's promise to rescue me becomes a reality. These moments encourage me to become more aware in times of struggle and in calm so that I may reach out to others in need and know that God is with us.

Deborah Meister

These (Busy) 'Days to Come'

In days to come... Isaiah 2:2

This is just what we're thinking about as Advent is underway, isn't it? All of the "days to come" from now until Christmas.

For many of us, the struggle will be the same we've gone through in years past—trying to hold the line against the pressures to entertain, to be entertained, to purchase gifts, to cook, to decorate. They are intense. We know we should be attending to our spiritual lives above all, preparing the way for the Lord in our own hearts... but when?

In days to come.

Notice what Isaiah says will happen "in days to come." Not: you will do things that will please others. Not: you will achieve and accomplish. Not: you will earn God's favor. No, in "days to come" God will give a great gift. Perhaps that clears a path through the busyness. In days to come, we might let go, listen and let God work wonders.

Lord, in days to come, fill my heart with joy.

Amy Welborn

December 4

The Pencil Sharpener

Blessed be the Lord, my rock,
    who trains my hands for battle, my fingers for war.

Psalm 144:1

In this psalm, David is acknowledging that his military successes have only come about because of God. My hands, while not trained for war, have been trained by God to serve him as a writer. When I have been confident enough to let it occur, I have often felt the Holy Spirit "training" my hands and guiding my fingers across the keyboard.

While I nearly exclusively use a keyboard now, I still have an affection for holding in my hands that most simple of writing implements—the pencil. I'll admit, it's frustrating when the tip becomes dull or breaks. You have to stop, no matter how busy you might be, get a sharpener and grind out a new, fresh point.

Good relationships require much the same. When a pencil breaks, we trust that it can be made right again. Do we have that same certainty when our relationship with God and others feels dulled or broken?

Terence Hegarty

That You Have Chosen Me

I have called you friends... It was not you who chose me, but I who chose you... John 15:15, 16

Of the many passages in Scripture revealing God's love for us, this one stands out in a special way for me. That Jesus chooses us, and that what he chooses us to be a friend, I find an astonishing revelation. The relationship of friend is much more personal than just a follower or believer. It suggests warm, valued mutuality.

Real friendship comes from an on-going sharing of life, both profound and light-hearted, in which we have come to know each other deeply. We have been together in emergency rooms and surprise birthday parties. Spending time together matters to us greatly.

Jesus, that you have chosen me for your own friend, inviting me to share your life as you share mine, is a precious window on your love. When I struggle to pray sometimes, if I remember you as friend, I feel myself relax. I can just spend time with you wherever I am right then.

Patricia Livingston

December 6

Follow the Leader

Then he said to all, "If anyone wishes to come after me, he must deny himself and take up his cross daily and follow me."
Luke 9:23

Quick, what's your cross?

Maybe your cross is a parent who doesn't appreciate all the caregiving and emotional and financial support you try to provide. Maybe your cross is a child or spouse engaged in destructive, addictive behaviors. Maybe your cross is a fondness for gossip or negativity or worry.

Crosses. They're all different, and we all have them. They seem almost unbearable to carry. It's tempting instead to indulge in pity parties about how cruel the world is. But rather than lie down and surrender to our crosses' weight and splinters, Jesus calls us to do what he did each and every day of his life on earth, never more visibly and painfully than on the way to his crucifixion—pick up that cross and follow. He's there every step of the way, offering to shoulder part of the burden—if we're willing to invite his aid.

Jesus, my weight and my heart are heavy. Please help me take up my cross.

Melanie Rigney

Praying for Our Light to Come

...a voice shall sound in your ears:
"This is the way; walk in it." Isaiah 30:21

I often walk early in the morning while it is still dark. It takes a while for my eyes to adjust to the darkness, but gradually I am able to find my way on the road with no problem. It amazes me how eyes adjust to darkness, taking in whatever little bit of light there may be.

The human heart suffers from its own darkness, but it, too, is capable of discernment so as to see us through. We are able to walk with confidence toward the light of God's love. It is the light that can never be extinguished, light that can give hope to whatever darkness we suffer through.

During Advent we await the coming of the Light of the world. Isaiah's words burn with hope and expectation. They are words to take to heart as we walk in the darkness of this life, for we can walk with the light of faith. When the path is hard to find because of a particularly dark time, pray for the light to come. God will send it, and a seeking heart will find it.

Fr. James Stephen Behrens

AN EXPERIENCE OF GOD'S RADIANCE

**Lift up your eyes on high
and see who has created these...** Isaiah 40:26

I made a pilgrimage to the Basilica of Our Lady of Guadalupe in Mexico City. In the center of the Church is the 478-year-old miraculous image of Our Lady on St. Juan Diego's tilma, a woven robe made primarily of cactus fibers. I was impressed with the daily throngs of the faithful—some of whom devoutly approach the Basilica on their knees over the hard stone.

What is less known is how Juan Diego, after having met the Mother of God, chose to spend his remaining years. He asked the bishop's permission to live as a hermit on the hill where Our Lady appeared to him. Why would he? Clearly, the experience changed his life dramatically and permanently. In Mary, he saw a reflection of God's radiance, as the moon reflects the sun. And then, he wanted to remain in solitude as close to that glory as possible.

Each day, you and I are exposed to little reflections of this same divine glory. May we open our eyes this day and see the radiance of the One who created us.

Msgr. Stephen J. Rossetti

TOO BUSY TO SEE GOD'S GLORIES

All of us, gazing with unveiled face on the glory of the Lord, are being transformed into the same image from glory to glory, as from the Lord who is the Spirit. 2 Corinthians 3:18

My mother recently had cataract surgery that lifted a cloudy veil from her eyes. Now she daily rejoices in seeing things that were long hidden from her sight.

What serves to veil our vision of God and the glories of God? Busyness can be a veil. We may rush from place to place so fast we do not see the rain fall or the robins teaching their young to fly. We may worry over the weeds in the garden so much that we do not contemplate the sugar pea sprout. We may be so engrossed in planning the future that we fail to walk in today's sunshine.

In his poem, "The Living Flame of Love," St. John of the Cross asks God to "tear through the veil of this sweet encounter." John pleads for God to remove the veil from the inner eye of his heart, that he might gaze on God's loveliness with intimacy. We, too, can occasionally cease our busyness and ask the Lord to remove the veil so that we might gaze on God and God's glory.

Carolyn Deitering-Ancell

LISTENING TO ONE'S TEACHER

> **Your ways, O Lord, make known to me;**
> **teach me your paths...** Psalm 25:4

The family-centered religious education program in my parish was studying the sacraments. When they came to Holy Orders, a sixth-grader in the group asked, "Why aren't there more vocations to the priesthood?" The insightful answer came from one of the women in the group who said, "There is so much noise today it's hard to hear God's voice."

Telemarketers, the media, the boss, the "surround sound" of cell-phone conversations, loud music all vie for our attention, shattering our peace and undermining our solitude. God does not shout very often; God whispers. How will we ever hear him in the din?

This Advent, let's make it a priority to make the space, find the means, get the earplugs to allow us to simply sit quietly with God from time to time. We don't even need prayers or words or conversation. All we need is a chance to listen for God's voice and to see the path open before us.

Heather Wilson

A CHURCH FOR ALL

Sing and rejoice, O daughter Zion! See, I am coming to dwell among you... Zechariah 2:14

Today the whole Church pauses in the midst of the Advent season and invites us to reflect on the feast of Our Lady of Guadalupe. Mary did not appear to the upper classes, but to an Indian of the lower class, and she spoke in the local native dialect. She told Juan Diego that every human being is important, because each is made in the image of God. She speaks to all who feel inferior.

Her message was to build a church, not in the center of culture, but "in the sticks"—where the poor live. So the Church must always be present where the people are, especially the poor and forgotten ones. As Mary said to this humble, Mexican peasant so beautifully: "My dear Juanito, let nothing discourage you, nothing depress you. Am I not here as your mother?" This feast and this message are not just for the Mexican people, not just for the Americas, but for all the world. Don't we all need a heavenly Mother?

Blessed Mother, pray for us.

Fr. Martin Pable, O.F.M. Cap.

WHERE DOES OUR PRAYER TAKE US?

**How beautiful upon the mountains
are the feet of him who brings glad tidings...** Isaiah 52:7

Rabbi Abraham Heschel participated in Martin Luther King, Jr.'s march for civil rights in March 1965. The 54-mile march from Selma to Montgomery, Alabama was grueling, often impeded by protestors. Afterward, Heschel wrote, "When I marched in Selma, I felt my legs were praying." Heschel's words remind us that prayer is not limited to a certain place—a church, a synagogue, a retreat center or a prayer corner. Prayer is not restricted to words or to internal movements of our heart. Prayer is not separate from the rest of our life either. It is intimately bound up with what we do all day.

If prayer is genuine, Heschel implies, it will take us places. It will inspire us to do things, to get involved with critical issues of our day. In that sense then, our whole body prays—our legs, feet, hands, eyes, ears, voice, mind, heart. Pay attention this week to where your legs or feet take you. (If you're in a wheelchair, where do your wheels take you?) Are your destinations fueled in part by your prayer?

Sr. Melannie Svoboda, S.N.D.

Losers and Winners

But first he must suffer greatly and be rejected by this generation. Luke 17:25

One of my favorite Beatles songs is a lesser known one titled, "I'm a Loser." I think of this tune more and more these days since I am now firmly in the throes of middle age. If I'm not losing my reading glasses, I'm losing my train of thought or forgetting why I entered a room. But that's far less painful than being rejected by my peers.

How often do we do the rejecting, chastising others by saying under our breath, "What a loser!"? Or we say, "At least I'm not as bad as that person!" It can make us feel better, at least temporarily. Other times, we even call ourselves losers. By the standards of his generation, Jesus was quite the loser—rejected by those in power, not affluent, dying a horrible, tortuous death after being publicly ridiculed as a criminal. We all suffer at times and maybe feel like losers. But the kingdom of God is among us, and ultimately, we are all winners if we turn to our suffering Savior.

King of Kings, may we remain in your kingdom forever.

Terence Hegarty

WE HAVE ENOUGH OF WHAT COUNTS

God is able to make every grace abundant for you, so that in all things, always having all you need, you may have an abundance for every good work. 2 Corinthians 9:8

If there is any message with which we are indoctrinated in our consumer culture it is that we never have "enough" of anything. We are always urged to acquire something more or something different, to purchase the latest commodities, the newest soap, clothing, videos, even plastic surgical procedures. So we purchase one more item and discover the following week that we still do not have enough.

This belief can even extend to our very selves: "I am not enough." Contrary to this message, God assures us that we are enough and that we do have enough of everything that counts: enough time, enough talents, enough beauty, enough goodness, enough grace. These gifts are available in such abundant quantities that we even have enough to give away in good works.

Lord, help me to appreciate the good gifts I have.

Sr. Ruth Marlene Fox, O.S.B.

Ordinary and Extraordinary

Jesus said to them, "Come, have breakfast." John 21:12

Before he died, my father hoarded incandescent light bulbs. At the time, they were marked for government-mandated extinction. After his death, my adult children and I divided up the several dozen boxes. Now, more than five years later, I held the last of Dad's light bulbs in my hand. It was the only one in the house, but I hesitated. As the only child who's dealt with a ton of property from all of her deceased relatives, I've nurtured an attitude of detachment at this point. But, oh that light bulb! This was different. It represented a connection with the quirks and personality of my father that nothing else—not his books, not his political collection—did. So it makes sense to me that Jesus was present to his friends in such an ordinary moment that morning, letting them know that he was with them, not through elaborate productions, but rather through that lovely, ordinary, unique moment of breakfast offered in love, grilled by his own hand.

Amy Welborn

Unity With Conviction

But that we may not offend them, go to the sea, drop in a hook, and take the first fish that comes up. Open its mouth and you will find a coin worth twice the temple tax.

Matthew 17:27

The early Christian communities had to find their way amidst cultures that were not Christian. In the gospel we hear about a problem that is not specifically ours today, but the solution applies in many current situations. The problem: Are Jewish Christians obligated to pay the temple tax? The solution: No. But pay it anyway, so as not to offend.

Some convictions may be put aside if it helps keep the peace by not offending others. Isn't this applicable within our families? In our neighborhoods? In our workplaces? Even among the nations? We should not abandon our convictions, but when possible, we may set them aside to achieve the greater good of peace.

Dear Lord, give us the courage to hold fast to our necessary convictions, the humility to compromise when possible and the wisdom to know the difference.

Paige Byrne Shortal

Prayer Without Pretense

Lord, do not trouble yourself, for I am not worthy to have you enter under my roof. Luke 7:6

There are guests for whom our house must sparkle and shine. And there are guests for whom we throw open the door to our everyday clutter and dust. These latter are usually friends and family who drop by often, maybe daily or several times a week. Perhaps for just a short visit each time. They are cherished people for whom no pretense is necessary. They know us and love us as we are.

Jesus is one of these cherished people. And our prayer time is like an ordinary visit amidst the everyday clutter and dust of our heart. Sometimes it's a quick chat. At other times, it is words spoken while working. Then there are those long, lingering, intimate conversations over a cup of tea, on the lazy front porch swing or cuddled on the worn-comfortable sofa before the fire. Times for sharing thoughts. Times for listening. Times for silence. All are nourishing. All are wondrous.

Jesus come, take my hand, enter my heart and let's talk, laugh, cry, share and be together.

Charlotte A. Rancilio

December 18

RECOVERING TREASURES

What woman having ten coins and losing one does not light a lamp and sweep the house, searching carefully until she finds it? Luke 15:8

Some years ago, I happened to look down at my engagement ring and saw a hole where a diamond had once sparkled. Since there were two diamonds to begin with, the loss was obvious. Frantically, I searched house and garden for the diamond—taking apart plumbing, sweeping under appliances, scanning tile grout. Nothing! Reluctantly, I gave up the search and replaced the gem. Weeks later, as I was removing cat fur from the broom, I saw an unmistakable sparkle. My reaction was one of amazement and joy—not because of the monetary value of the diamond, but because, against all odds, I had recovered something precious to me. I had the ring reset with the three diamonds forming a triangle, a symbolic reminder to me.

If lost and found diamonds, coins, sheep and younger sons give rise to such joy, how much more should we celebrate the recovery of spiritual treasures? Such treasures as the ability to love, to hope, to feel compassion, to take risks, and to respond to God's call!

Elizabeth-Anne Vanek

BROTHERS AND SISTERS

You, Judah, shall your brothers praise...
the sons of your father shall bow down to you.

Genesis 49:8

Ah, the family dynamic! Imagine the mood of Judah's brothers, being told by their father that they will bow down to Judah. These are the same men who, years earlier, took part in one of the most famous cases of sibling rivalry ever. Their brother, Joseph, had dreamt that they would bow to him. So filled with resentment at the idea were Joseph's brothers, that they plotted to kill him. Instead, they only sold him into slavery.

They must have been more receptive to being led by Judah. After all, they had recently reunited with Joseph, who was now able to save them from starvation because he was where God wanted him to be.

Can we learn to let go of our resentments, humble ourselves and trust that divine providence is at work in us and in others? Maybe we can start by trusting that God resides in each of us, including all of our brothers and sisters.

Terence Hegarty

DECEMBER 20

LOVE NOTES FROM GOD

In the day of my distress I call upon you, for you will answer me. Psalm 86:7

I was feeling sad, close to tears. My morning prayer had not helped. I kept thinking of my dear ones now dead. I thought especially of my husband, his strength, his loving concern, his humor. I was very lonely.

I stopped on my way to work to buy some fruit for lunch. I literally bumped into one of the deacons from our church. He had the same first name as my husband. After greeting me, he quite spontaneously told me he had been thinking of me and I was in his prayers. God had heard my unvoiced cry of distress and sent the deacon to let me know that God loves me and is always with me.

These things happen to all of us and we must be alert to recognize the source. God is always sending messages of love and tenderness, a balm to soothe the bruised heart.

I went on my way with a lightened step, a glow of love and thanks for my Father's loving concern.

Joan Zrilich

WITH THOSE WHOM YOU LOVE

> The Lord said…, "Martha, Martha, you are anxious and worried about many things. There is need of only one thing. Mary has chosen the better part and it will not be taken from her."
>
> Luke 10:41-42

My mother was a Martha. At holiday meals, with siblings long-moved-away visiting for just a few hours, she would flit back and forth to the kitchen. "Don't worry about that. Just sit with us!," we would say. She would smile anxiously and return to her work.

Martha is busy doing the right things, being good. Mary just stays with Jesus, soaking it in. And, of course, Martha is resenting Mary to no end. *Oh sure, she can enjoy herself because I'm doing all the work!* She even asks Jesus to rebuke Mary for it. It takes quite a stretch, which many have strained to make, to misunderstand Jesus' simple scolding of Martha—"Mary has chosen the better part."

We're all part Martha and part Mary. And, while both are needed, try not to be so busy that you miss the opportunity to stop and be with those whom you love.

Phil Fox Rose

'Care of Souls'

Take care…not to forget the things which our eyes have seen…but teach them to your children and to your children's children. Deuteronomy 4:9

We are responsible for the formation of our children, but how tempting it is to turn over this important work to someone else. I'm tempted despite my two degrees in theology and years of pastoral work. I fear that mine are like the barefoot children of the shoemaker.

Raising good, faith-filled, prayerful, knowledgeable Christian children is challenging, but holy work. How can we do it better? Perhaps there are little changes that could be made—the music we listen to at home and in our cars; the shows we watch; the books we read. Perhaps prayers before meals and at bedtime could be more substantial. We could be more faithful about Mass together or attend a communal penance service. Take a field trip to a nearby shrine or cathedral or a religious order's public Sunday Mass.

This work is called the "care of souls." What higher priority could we possibly have?

Paige Byrne Shortal

REJOICING AGAIN

Once more will he fill your mouth with laughter, and your lips with rejoicing. Job 8:21

For a while when the kids were young, it seemed like I was always angry. Someone always needed correction or consequences, and I forgot how to just enjoy their company. I thought I needed to present a veneer of constant vigilance and authority or I'd lose control of my environment.

A long-time friend pointed out that anger was never my default position as a child. She had been there when we were kids, and it's true, we used to get very silly and laugh in a way I never have since.

Part of the joy of childhood is trusting that we belong to someone and will be cared for. Our parents fulfill this role for us when we're young. But, as adults, we still need to know that we belong to someone. Otherwise, we are tempted to usurp all the authority and judgment that should be left to God. Anyone would buckle under that weight.

It takes a radical readjustment of trust to believe that God will handle his own personal relationship with each of our children— just as he has with us. But it is cause for rejoicing!

Elizabeth Duffy

Christmas Always

And this will be a sign for you: you will find an infant wrapped in swaddling clothes and lying in a manger. Luke 2:12

I confess, I sometimes sympathize with the Grinch. I look for ways to stop Christmas from coming. The closer it gets, the more trouble I have finding signs of anything except materialism, nihilism and human loss. I desire to flee.

Fortunately, God doesn't think the way I do! He doesn't run away from us; he comes to find us. He doesn't condemn us, but looks for the good and the true in us. He finds it too. Truth is, love and kindness are everywhere, if we are small and still enough to recognize them.

The sign God gives is so simple and quiet, it could easily be lost in the busyness of commerce—except it's not. Over the centuries, this sign has spoken to human hearts continually. Here's the answer to human longing, given without conditions or condemnations. As often as we overlook that answer, God offers it again. Christmas doesn't happen once a year; it's with us always, as God is with us, forever, unconditionally.

Mary Marrocco

Famous Last Words

Lord Jesus, receive my spirit. Acts 7:59

These last words of St. Stephen, the first martyr, are a beautiful expression of his unwavering faith. As Catholics, we pray for a beautiful death. Being brutally killed doesn't fit our understanding of that, but Stephen's was a beautiful death because his faith remained strong. We'd like to imagine passing away when we are quite elderly, surrounded by loving family members. We'd offer tear-filled good-byes and, like Stephen, ask God to receive our spirit. Yet many do not get such an opportunity. Our Savior, whose birth we joyously celebrate in this season, was murdered at age 33. People have heart attacks; kindergartners succumb to cancer. And, still today, people are martyred.

Perhaps in advance of our final moments, keeping our newborn Savior in mind, we can attempt to build our own unwavering faith by regularly offering a modified version of the prayer that Stephen uttered.

Lord Jesus, I humbly pray that at the hour of my death, you will receive my spirit.

Terence Hegarty

December 26

RETURN TO TRANQUILITY

> Return, O my soul, to your tranquility,
> for the LORD has been good to you.
> For he has freed my soul from death,
> my eyes from tears, my feet from stumbling.
> I shall walk before the LORD
> in the lands of the living. Psalm 116:7-9

My soul is often un-tranquil, tormented by thoughts of how I want my life to be, of how I would arrange things if I controlled the universe. Frustration, anger, hurt swirl within as I nurse my disappointment.

The Spirit calls my soul to return to tranquility, to sit before God in silence, to remember the many, many gifts the Lord has given me. How many times I have been saved, comforted, lifted up from failure and despair! I remember the small gifts of today, the beauty of a sunset or the kind word received. I remember the many joys of years past, the holidays, the reunions, the triumphs. I remember when I have walked with God through hard times and through celebrations. And I give thanks. And I know that the kingdom begins here, in the land of the living and that if I remember that God is with me here, I will walk with tranquility.

Denise Barker

ASK AND RECEIVE

While it is true that I neither fear God nor respect any human being, because this widow keeps bothering me I shall deliver a just decision for her... Luke 18:4-5

Years ago, I started making a list of answered prayers. When I read down the list now, I am surprised to see favors recorded that I have totally forgotten about. Some were trifling, but important to me at the time. Others were more significant: a friend who was restored to health, an alcoholic who stopped drinking.

God my Father is not like the unjust judge who took care of the widow's needs simply to be rid of her. My Father, Jesus tells me, will not delay. As soon as he knows my needs he will be there to help me.

This doesn't mean that I expect everything that I ask for will be granted. My Father knows what I need better than I know myself, and I trust his decisions. In the meantime, my list reminds me of the many times God has answered my prayers. As I present new petitions to my Father, I do it with heartfelt thanks.

Lord, you have encouraged your people to come to you with their petitions. We humbly present them before you, knowing you will not delay.

Mary Best

December 28

CRAVING SPIRITUAL GOODS

I have never wanted anyone's silver or gold or clothing.

Acts 20:33

I wish I could say with St. Paul that I have never been envious. But that sneaky little sin often creeps up on me when I am observing a finer house, sportier car or nicer outfit than my own. It depends, I guess, on where one has set one's heart. If it is set in the ways of the world, it will crave the better things of the world, the things that are said to bring security, admiration, pleasure. But if the heart can be tuned to the ways of the spirit, then it will crave the goods of the spirit—peace, wisdom and the joy that passes all understanding. And one never need envy the riches of the kingdom because the more they are shared with others, the more they multiply. There is always enough for all.

If we fill our lives with the compassion of Christ, the creative energy of the Father, the freedom and joy of the Spirit, good companions on the journey and the nourishment of Scripture and the Eucharist, our hearts will never need to be envious or want for anything.

Denise Barker

To Keep and to Ponder

And his mother kept all these things in her heart. Luke 2:51

Twice Luke says Mary "kept in her heart" the events surrounding Jesus' birth and growth (2:19, 51), once with the "keeping" linked to "pondering." These two responses might well be seen as ultimately the only way for us humans to approach family life and the life of faith. How often in family life and in the life of faith are we left with little else except what we keep and ponder in our hearts?

We keep and ponder because we do not understand all that happens. We keep and ponder because we do not fully understand our spouses or our children—or even ourselves. Life is a mystery— and family life is an even more profound mystery! You do not ever resolve the bittersweet realities of family life. You just "keep them in your heart" and rock them back and forth. We keep and ponder in our spiritual lives, also, because with God, the Ultimate Mystery, nothing can ever be final, nothing can be resolved or concluded. Much as we might want only answers, in this life we must keep and ponder questions in our hearts.

James E. Adams

December 30

Passing on the Faith

The Lord is good:
his kindness endures forever,
and his faithfulness, to all generations. Psalm 100:5

The word "generations" brings to my mind a whole series of people lined up behind me whose past has helped to shape the person I am today. I know a great deal about my parents, less about my grandparents and scarcely anything about my great grandparents and others who stretch back into history. I often wonder about my ancestors who first accepted Jesus Christ and so began a procession of people who passed on their faith from one generation to the next until my parents handed it on to me. Some of them must have found themselves in tragic circumstances. Yet the words of the psalmist were on their lips and in their hearts: "The Lord is good. God's kindness endures forever..."

Today I belong to the generation receiving God's untold blessings. Even though I may walk in a dark valley at times, I know by faith that God is with me and I can acknowledge God's kindness with the words of this psalm. I pray that I will be a credit to those who have passed these words on to me, and that I, in turn, will teach the next generation to have them in their hearts and on their lips.

Mary Best

PRAYERS

MORNING PRAYERS

Lord of heaven and earth, by your power and for your glory, the sun has come up another day. Thank you for the gift of life renewed throughout the universe. I offer this day to you. May all that I do, say and think be for your greater glory. AMEN.

Good and gracious God, a new day dawns for us and with it comes another opportunity to do your will in the world. Help me to understand the role I am to play today in your continuing drama of salvation. Help me to live one day at a time, free of the burdens of the past and of the fear of the future. Give me patience, generosity and kindness in my relationships with those you have placed in my life. Keep me close to you all the day long. AMEN.

Good Shepherd, some mornings sleep lingers, a fog remains, and I hesitate to welcome the day. While I do not know what's in store for me today, help me, I pray, to appreciate the bounty that you have laid before me. Awaken my faith, lift the fog, lead me in your ways that I might go forward confidently, knowing that you go before me. AMEN.

Heavenly Father, I thank you for the dawn of a new day. Through the life-giving power of your Holy Spirit, you have given me another opportunity to grow in faith, hope and love by serving you and my neighbor. Guide me in my work today, and show me how to bear fruit and find joy in all that I do. Help me to become the person you want me to be so that I can reveal your love to others.

Amen.

O my God! I offer thee all my actions of this day for the intentions and for the glory of the Sacred Heart of Jesus. I desire to sanctify every beat of my heart, my every thought, my simplest works, by uniting them to its infinite merits; and I wish to make reparation for my sins by casting them into the furnace of its Merciful Love. O my God! I ask of thee for myself and for those whom I hold dear, the grace to fulfill perfectly thy Holy Will, to accept for love of thee the joys and sorrows of this passing life, so that we may one day be united together in heaven for all eternity. Amen.

St. Thérèse of Lisieux
Notre Dame Book of Prayer

The Lord's acts of mercy are not exhausted, his compassion is not spent; They are renewed each morning—great is your faithfulness! The Lord is my portion, I tell myself, therefore I will hope in him.

Lamentations 3:22-24

EVENING PRAYERS

Good Shepherd, you have led me to the end of another day. Help me to look back over the hours that have passed since I woke up this morning. Show me the times when I could have responded better to the promptings of your Holy Spirit. Show me, too, the times I experienced your presence, whether I was aware of it at the time. Lord, I offer you this night in the hope that I might be strengthened and renewed to serve you tomorrow. AMEN.

Lord, you invited your disciples to watch and pray with you in the garden on the night before you suffered. If I am wakeful tonight and unable to sleep, be with me as I turn to watch and pray with you. Whether in prayer or sleep, may I be restored for the day's work ahead. AMEN.

Your gift of nighttime is here, O Lord. I thank you in advance for keeping me and those whom I love far from sin and close to you, this night and all of our days and nights to come. AMEN.

Good and gracious God, thank you for this day with all its blessings and challenges. Pardon me for the times I closed my heart to your presence and missed an opportunity to be a channel of your love. For the times your presence brought me light and a gentle spirit, I thank you. May I sleep well tonight, trusting in your unending care for me and those I love. AMEN.

O my God, fill my soul with holy joy, courage and strength to serve You. Enkindle Your love in me and then walk with me along the next stretch of road before me. I do not see very far ahead, but when I have arrived where the horizon now closes down, a new prospect will open before me and I shall meet with peace. AMEN.

St. Teresa Benedicta of the Cross (Edith Stein)

A PRAYER FOR THE GIFT OF THE BLESSED MOTHER

Lord Jesus, you gave your mother Mary to the Church to encourage us to persevere in tough times. Instill in us now the desire to draw near to her and receive her motherly care. The first to bear you into the world, may she continue to inspire us to follow you in humility and openness to the workings of the Holy Spirit. May we always realize that our devotion to her will never lead us astray but always point us back to you. Help us take to heart her words to the wine stewards at the wedding feast at Cana: "Do whatever he tells you." AMEN.

A PRAYER TO GUARD AGAINST DEPRESSION

O Christ Jesus, when all is darkness and we feel our weakness and helplessness, give us the sense of your presence, your love and your strength. Help us to have perfect trust in your protecting love and strengthening power, so that nothing may frighten or worry us, for, living close to you, we shall see your hand, your purpose, your will through all things.

St. Ignatius of Loyola

A PRAYER FOR LENT

Lord Jesus, you became a servant to show us the path to true greatness. We pray that through our Lenten prayer and practice, your Holy Spirit may shape us into true disciples capable of serving you and our sisters and brothers. Give us the strength and courage to put your words into practice each day. Help us to recognize our sin and whatever is holding us back from you. Make us willing to change so that we can be the people you are creating us to be.

Amen.

A PRAYER FOR THE EASTER SEASON

Resurrected Lord, like Mary Magdalene who searched for you in the tomb, we can despair of finding you in our lives. Then, so overwhelmed by our own private griefs, we do not recognize you when you are right in front of us. Help us throughout this holy season of Easter to become more deeply aware of your presence in our lives. May we eagerly accept the new life you offer us each moment. Open our hearts to your love as we seek to understand and embrace the meaning of the Resurrection in a fresh, vibrant way. Amen.

A PRAYER FOR MOTHERS

Loving God, with caring embraces, wisdom and guidance, a mother prepares her children to give their gifts to the world. Grant mothers patience and courage as they do the hard work of lovingly raising children and of lovingly guiding their adult children. May they have hope amid the world's turmoil and may they trust in your eternal care for each one of us. Amen.

A PRAYER FOR FATHERS

God, send your blessing down on all fathers, especially my own, whom I now recall with great gratitude. Strengthen all the world's fathers so that they might give their children the love and protection that they need to become the girls and boys, men and women that you call them to be. Amen.

A PRAYER FOR ADVENT

Dear Jesus, may the illuminated Advent wreath remind us of you, the Light of the World. Help us to open our hearts, our homes and our family to your eternal light and peace. AMEN.

A PRAYER FOR CHRISTMAS

Almighty God, born a tiny baby in Bethlehem, you trusted Mary and Joseph to make you a safe, loving home. May we likewise trust in you for every good thing. You embraced our humanity in order to give us a share of your divine life. May we acknowledge you as our Creator and accept the first of your life within us. In Jesus, you gave us hope of life without end. May we give you praise, glory and thanksgiving in this Christmas season. AMEN.

A PRAYER FOR THE NEW YEAR

Lord, I am very grateful for the times I can see your hand at work in my life, the moments I can feel your presence and sense your love for me. But for those other times, I pray, dear Lord, that I might have unquenchable trust in you. When I cannot see where my life is headed or how all things work for good for those who love you, I ask for trust that you are in charge. AMEN.

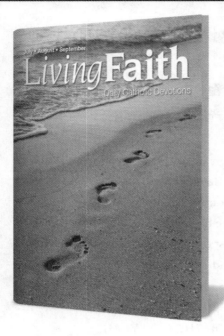
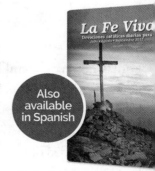

ough **Daily Catholic Devotions**

Grow young hearts in faith too!

Each issue is perfect for kids and includes:

- Devotions based on the daily Scripture readings
- Full-color illustrations

Fun activities including:

- Games and puzzles
- Saints, seasons and much more

Ideal for ages 6-12

KIDS 4" X 6"
$16 per year

With brief but profound spiritual gems each day,
Living Faith will become a cherished part
of your faith life.